My Crooked Path
by Peter Paddon

My Crooked Path

by Peter Paddon

PENDRAIG PUBLISHING, Los Angeles

Pendraig Publishing, Sunland, CA 91040
© 2009 Peter Paddon. All rights reserved.
Published 2009
Printed in the United states of America

ISBN: 978-0-9843302-0-1

Table of Contents

Introduction

It really is funny how projects can take on a life of their own. When I started the Crooked Path podcast, I had no idea on how to do it, what to include, or even whether anyone would bother to listen. I just sat down and recorded some stuff, then figured out how to set up an rss feed, the proper format for the mp3 file, and so on. It was all trial and error, and not at all taken seriously. My original intent was to do something that would give me an opportunity to promote my DVDs.

But I guess the universe had other plans. I got hooked on podcasting pretty quickly, which is kind of ironic as, even to this day, I'm not one for listening to podcasts. I listen to occasional podcasts by my friends, or if someone points me at an episode that has something relevant to me, but other than that, generally not. It is probably because, between the books, DVDs, the journal and my own podcast (and video podcast, when I get time to do one), I don't really have time to sit down and listen, to do a spoken word podcast justice.

So anyway, fast forward a few years, and I've just put my 112th episode on the website, and the book you hold in your hands is in the process of being put together. The hardest part is getting the whole thing transcribed... 100 episode at around 40 minutes per episode is a lot of audio to be transcribed at a dollar a minute. I don't have $4000 to spare – let's face it, I don't have $4000 period! So I turned to the people who listen to the podcast. Over 1000 people are registered at the Crooked Path website (www.crookedpath.org), and two or three times that number listen to the podcast itself, and luckily, a few of them were willing to tackle the job, one episode at a time. So I would like to thank Stephen Rose especially, for transcribing most of the episodes included in this book, and also Marie Dill and Ashley Roff, for transcribing the rest of them.

Of course, there was a little more work to be done. I get the pleasure of editing each transcript, both to correct errors, and to change some of my rambling into more reader-friendly text. Finally, I add a few notes where necessary for context and clarity, and away we go.

Over the last three years, I've experimented a bit with the format. The early podcasts really had no format, just me rambling on about my topic of the day, but I finally settled into a format of sorts, where I start off covering a subject's lore, and then in the second half, I go over some practical aspect of the topic at hand.

Somewhere along the way I had the genius idea of asking my friend and initiator, Raven Womack, to add a section on wortcunning, or herb-lore, in the middle. This proved to be very popular, and she has been described as Janice Joplin on herbs! I've also occasionally included music, most often from Wendy Rule, who is still one of the few Pagan musicians I've found that I consistently like the stuff she puts out – as I write this, I'm in the process of setting up a concert for her here in Los Angeles for the second time (I did it last year too), for the start of her 2009 US tour.

I've also had interviews with notable characters from the Pagan community – controversial ones too. Robin Artisson is notorious in his own right, and even Orion Foxwood has his detractors, but the biggest stir was when I interviewed Dave Finnin of the clan of Tubal Cain. It was a total surprise when I was contacted by Shani Oates, the self-proclaimed "Maid of Tubal Cain", who lambasted me for "not doing my research". She was even more incensed when I interviewed Carol and Blackthorn, another Maid and Magister duo from the Tubal Cain stable.

Ironically, I would have been happy to interview Shani as well, because despite knowing Ann and Dave Finnin for years, I truly do not have a stake in anyone's legitimacy. But she was so belligerent, childish and dogmatic that in the end I would not have done it, even if she had been willing. That particular debacle continues to this day, fueled by the entry into the fray by others with their own less than honorable agendas. In fact, the on-going saga is a large part of my decision around Midsummer to discontinue the podcast and the website, though I am still podcasting in a slightly different format at the Pendraig website.

So here we are. In your hands lies the wit and wisdom (or folly and foolishness, depending on your perspective) of a selection of episodes from the first year or so of The Crooked Path. No doubt, should this prove to be a popular book, there will be a second volume. In the meantime, please enjoy the fruits of my fevered mind.

Peter Paddon
Lammas 2009

The path of the Outcast
Episode 0, broadcast March 1, 2006

Hello and welcome to a very special episode of the Crooked Path. My name is Peter Paddon and what you are about to hear is the pilot episode of the Crooked Path, which I recorded earlier in the year to test out the technology. It's a good one. It's the path of the outcast. I hope you enjoy it.

I thought it might be interesting to talk about the path of the outcast. Now this was inspired by a discussion topic that I saw on a web site Pagan life, Paganlife.net, which is an excellent Pagan community. The majority of its members are in the UK, but there's some from Canada and the US as well. It's very lively, with very intelligent conversations, and I've been really enjoying it, so I heartily recommend it to anybody who wants to actually get into some good conversations. Anyway, somebody mentioned that they were getting this strange feeling of isolation, which is something that I've had to deal with a lot myself. So I thought I'd talk about it a little bit, in the hopes that we can stop people from worrying about it too much. 'Cause it's going to be there forever.

What we're talking about is this sense of being isolated, of being alone even when you're in a crowd, even when within a crowd of Pagans, you'll sit apart from them. You feel like there's something between you and them that stops you from being a part of it. You feel very much alone. And it can be very disconcerting, especially when you're not sure where it's coming from.

So what causes this, because it seems to be a very universal experience that people have as they get deeper into a Pagan or magical path. And there are some very practical reasons for why this should occur. The first of these is that if you're following a magical path, you're going through experiences that can only be shared with others who have already been there before you, because nobody else would really understand. There's also experiences that you just don't have the words to explain, that even somebody else who's been there you can't really talk about either, because you can't find the words. You just have to hope that they've been there enough that they know what you're trying to say and get the gist of it that way. And then of course there's, if you have friends who aren't Pagan, if you talk to them about your experiences, they're going think you're a little flakey.

Even those who are Pagan friendly may not really understand what you're talking about, and may make light of it, or make you feel like uncomfortable in some way - without meaning to, of course. And this can get really, really depressing. I've known people who've had a terrible time, and this isn't something that goes away. I think I should warn you about this. I've been following this Pagan path for over twenty years now, and I still get it.

The thing is, even people who are Pagan don't always understand it, if they're not going into it as deeply as you are. You see, our path is tailored to us. We tailor it to suit our own needs. So even when we're in a coven or some other kind of group, it's still really just a bunch of individuals who happen to be traveling in the same direction for a while. It's a bit like caravanning or car pooling on a road trip. You didn't start out with these people. You may not end up with these people. But right now you all happen to be going to the same place at the same time. And so you travel together for convenience. But you're still very much an individual travelling along your own path.

There are also some magical reasons for this. Most people who practice a Pagan belief system, at the very least, work with meditation, altered states of consciousness. Those who follow a magical path, can add to this practices such as walking between the worlds, astral travel, and other ways of actively exploring the realms. There's old term for people who do this sort of thing. They used to be called hedge-walkers or hedge-riders. Until fairly recently - the last hundred and fifty years or so ago - in the UK, movement from place to place was very restricted for common folk. Only the gentry, tinkers, and craftsmen could travel from place to place without permission from the lord of the manner. Craftsmen, of course, included healers, cunning folk and the like. In other words, people like us.

Magical folk, metaphorically and sometime literally, live on the outskirts of society. Most find it hard to relate to non-magical folk. Right from the beginning, that's how they end up getting into a Pagan or magical life style - because they finally found they could find people that they could relate to.

And as they get deeper into their studies, they find this difficulty becomes much more pronounced. For example, as I said, I've been doing this Pagan magical stuff for over twenty years now, and I remember back in high school when I found it very difficult to understand why people didn't seem to be the way I was. I had a lot of trouble with people being selfish, petty, materialistic. I never really understood why. I mean, I had a generalized spirituality of my own, which other people didn't seem to bother with. And it was very, very confusing for me.

Finally, when I became a Pagan and started practicing, I found that there were other people, in fact, who had the same thoughts and feelings along those lines as I did, which made me feel a lot better. But even then, every now and then it would crop up that I felt that I was different or I was alone. There was a barrier between me and the rest of the rest of humanity. And it got very disconcerting. This has happened, off and on, all the way through to the last couple of years when I really started to explore and understand what was going on for me, courtesy of the tradition that I now follow, where they actually recognized that this happens and start to teach you to deal with it.

You can't get rid of it but you can learn to handle it: and the way you handle it is when you need to be alone, you go and be alone, and nobody bugs you for it. So that's really what it's all about. Even now, as I said, I'm following the tradition I've been searching for all of my life. I'm very, very lucky in that sense, yet end even now, in the middle of a crowd of people who are all in my tradition, I can find myself going off and having some quiet time by myself, because I need to be apart, because I feel apart and alone. It's just one of those things. As I said, it doesn't go away. But knowing that other people are going through the same thing makes it a little easier to manage.

So, what are the benefits of this? I mean, if you've drawn the shitty card of being alone and on the edge of society as an out-cast, why? What's the point of it all? There must be some ben-efit to it, otherwise people would have stopped doing it a long time ago, and there wouldn't be any Pagans or magical people anymore. Well, people drawn to this path usually have a vora-cious appetite for learning. On a purely practical level, it's eas-ier to indulge this in solitude. As I said before, those of us who are part of a thriving Pagan community appreciate the gathering of like minded folk. But we will take ourselves away from time to time to work with the solitude. We can have too much even of our own type of people.

You see, those who are initiated into a tradition of any sort, be it Gardnerian Wicca, Alexandrian Wicca, any other sort of Wicca or Traditional Witchcraft or any other magical path, are twice born. They're set apart in the same way that the chosen people, the Hebrew consider themselves set apart by God. This auto-matically puts up a barrier between us and mundane folk. We're different, which is why we begin to mix only with those who are like us. Because it's easier to mix with people where there's less of a barrier. It's just human nature.

Besides, as we become more deeply involved, our beliefs, our values, and our ideas of good conduct change. Suddenly an evening swilling beer and watching sports just doesn't cut it anymore. I'm sure anybody who's been following this path for a little while has found that there are things that the people who they associate with out of habit do, that they just can't understand the point of anymore.

Unfortunately, this is a subject that's not often spoken about. So people experiencing it for the first time find themselves without a frame of reference. They don't know what the hell's going on, and it disturbs them. They decide that because they're feeling like an outsider, it's because they don't belong on the path, and then they leave it to find out what they do belong to. The trouble is, of course, that if you do belong on this path and walk away from it, you're still going to carry away the isolation and the sense of apartness with you. But on top of that you're going to add the stresses and trauma of not being true to yourself.

That's the main reason why I decided to talk about this subject today. In the hopes that those of you that are experiencing this side of the path, will recognize it for what it is, the calling to walk between worlds, to mediate as priesthood, to become the wise woman or cunning man. The knowledge of why you feel this way won't stop you feeling it. But you can draw ironic comfort that you are not alone in your isolation, that every true Witch feels it. It ebbs and flows. Sometimes you feel it more than other times. But remember, it is part of the mark of the witch. And it's the coin you pay in exchange for amazing experiences you have between the worlds. Yes, those same experiences that you just can't share with any but a select few.

Sacred Space and Ancestral Work
Episode 3, broadcast March 6, 2006

Hello, and welcome to the Crooked Path. I'm your host Peter Paddon. And today we're going to be taking a look at ancestral work. But first, let's talk about sacred space.

Sacred space means different things to different people. So really, the only way I can get around that is to tell you what it means to me. Sacred space is an enclosure we create, if you like, an artificial bubble in mundane reality, inside which we create an environment that is conducive to whatever type of ritual work or crafting work we plan on doing.

Now there's a lot of different methods in different traditions on creating sacred space. A lot of different names too. For the average NeoPagan Wiccan, circle casting is the term that springs to mind. But circle casting is not exactly what the traditional Witch or cunning folk or traditional crafter would call the setting up of their sacred space. The reason for this is down to good old fashion history, and the fact that Crafters are not likely to use terms that have been borrowed from other places.

You see, circle casting is technically a ceremonial magic technique, and as Wicca borrowed quite a lot of its ritual structure from ceremonial magic, from the Golden Dawn, courtesy of Gerald Gardener and even more so Alex Sanders, who got even more ceremonial than Gerald did. So the circle casting that you have in most Wiccan covens is very ceremonial oriented. It uses the classical elements, or the Watch Towers as they're often called. Even the phrase that is used when drawing the circle, in Gardnerian and Alexandrian circles at least, is taken straight out of the Key of Solomon: "I conjure thee, o circle of power, that thou be'est a boundary between the world of men and the realms of the mighty ones; a guardian

17

and protection that shall preserve and contain the power that I shall raise within thee. Wherefore do I bless thee in the names of the Lord and Lady", or words to that effect.

So, it's very much about creating a barrier, a boundary within which you can work. And perhaps the most significant difference from the point of view of a crafter between the ceremonial or Wiccan circle and the sacred space created by non-Wiccan methods is that in a Wiccan circle, in a ceremonial circle, the aim is to set up an environment. And then bring everything you need into that environment. So you call upon your deities and bring them into the circle with you. Drawing down the Moon, drawing down the Sun, invoking, bringing things in. This is very much the modus operandi of the ceremonial magician. He stays put and everything comes to him or her.

In traditional crafting, it actually works the other way around. The space is warded, or set aside if you like. And then the crafter takes the space and themselves to where ever it is the entities or energies that they want to work with happen to be. So, there's a definite difference in feel, if nothing else. There's also a difference in names.

Most traditional crafters try to avoid saying "casting circle" unless they really have to, just because they want to emphasize the fact that it's different from what a Wiccan does. Names that you might find being used for creating sacred space, warding the space, laying a compass, plowing the bloody acre, raising the hedgerow, lot's of different terms like that, which tend to be very physical-sounding descriptive terms. And each of them has a particular technique associated with it.

Some are use predominantly by a particular tradition, and some are more generic. Warding the space is probably the most generic term. It covers all the techniques for doing this. And it just involves essentially - and there are traditional crafters that are going to hate me saying this - casting a circle by another name. It is making the space in which you're standing something special, set aside from the mundane world.

Laying a Compass is a little bit more technical than just warding space, because what you're aiming to do is to set out the lie of the land, which is a very old fashioned sort of phrase, but it involves basically setting out things that are specific to your tradition and establishing their relationship to each other within the space and placing yourself in the center or fulcrum-point, so that you're able to bring about the changes that you want.

And it takes a little bit of practice. Laying the Compass is not something you can learn from a book. It's something you really have to either get a light bulb moment about, or have somebody who is skilled at it work you through it. Like most traditional crafting techniques, it's all very experiential. You have to actually learn it hands on. So I'm not going to try to explain it in detail here, except basically what you're trying to do is you're trying to superimpose your tradition's map of the universe upon the land upon which you're working.

Plowing the bloody acre is more of an outdoor term. It often involves the traditional image of dragging your left leg or your right leg, usually left leg, as you work your way around the perimeter of the circle space to establish a boundary marker, if you like. And the bloody acre is the area that is covered by the river of blood. It's a nice technical term, as used in fairy faith as well as several other old crafting traditions, that it's basically the current of magic or crafting that the practitioner is part of, so you're talking about immersing yourself in the current, in the tradition itself.

"Plowing" is working the land quite literally, and making the two one and the same, because all traditions, all currents come out of the land in one form or another, because they're tied into the Ancestors which we'll be talking about later.

So do we do this indoors or outdoors? Well, as I was taught, if you can't work your magic stark naked in a concrete bunker, then you can't work magic period. So ultimately it doesn't matter. But obviously sometimes you're going to be working indoors and sometimes you're going to be working outdoors. Does the technique change? Yes it does, mainly because traditional crafters tend to see all of the land outdoors as sacred to a greater or lesser extent. So you don't really need to make the land sacred - it's already that.

So when working outdoors, you just basically set up your boundary markers and you do your work, and usually at the end of it, rather than taking it all down again, you just walk away from it, because you're not going to desanctify the land, any more than you're going to make it more sacred than it started out to be.

Indoors is a different matter. If you work in a temple, then you're going to build up a similar sort of effect over the years in your temple space as well. But if you have to use the living room or a corner of your bedroom, then you're basically going to put it up and take it down each time as completely as you can so that you don't have any issues with using that space for mundane purposes at other times. So that's basically the bare nuts and bolts of sacred space. Of course, once you're in it and you've got it established there's a whole world of topics we can discuss on what you can do when you're in there. But we'll save that for another time.

And so, we're on to the Ancestors. So, who am I talking about when I refer to Ancestors? Obviously, the thing that springs to mind is grandma and grandpa and all of their kith and kin. But, hopefully we're going back a little further than that.

"Ancestors" is a word that get thrown around a lot, and I don't know if everybody really sits and thinks about what they mean when they say it. We're obviously not just talking about grandparents, great grandparents and aunts and uncles and so on and so forth when we're talking about ancestors. We're going back a little further than that, and referring to the pre-Christian ancestors who did the sort of things that we're hoping to reconstruct, recreate, recover, whatever phrase you want to use for it.

It really is meant to mean your blood ancestors, but in practice we're really talking about the ancestors of our race or our species. We tend to cast the net a little wider. We'll take anybody from way back when who has a nugget of lore or information that they want to share with us. So, we're really not that proud when it comes to stuff like that. We'll take it from anywhere. Ancestors are generally very important parts of traditional crafting. It's probably one of the biggest things that differentiates traditional craft from Wicca is the focus on ancestral workings. Garderian and Alexandrian Wicca does have ancestral workings, but they're not as well known or as obvious in most cases. But they do exist. But ancestral work within the Traditional Crafting community - if you can call it a community: a bunch of ornery individuals that I don't know if the word community applies here - but ancestors play a very important part in both the Wheel of the Year, rites of the year, and also the personal crafting of a Traditional Crafter.

So, it's important to get your bearings where the ancestors are concerned. Really, they are a very key component of most rituals and of the current of the Tradition in general. Obviously, they're seen in some mythic sense as being the progenitors of the tradition. And probably one of the most obvious signs of ancestral working in a coven or group will be some sort of stone and probably some sort of representation of a skull upon the altar at some point. On our altar we have a large hearth stone. And we have a pewter skull with Celtic markings sitting on top of that to represent our Ancestors.

I should point out at this point that the use of an altar itself is almost considered blasphemy in some traditional crafting circles. We happen to have a table that I made specially for the purpose of putting stuff on when we're working ritual. So technically, it's an altar. But it's more of a work table than place of worship. We don't do any bowing of the head and that sort of stuff there, at least, not when anyone's looking. We call upon the Ancestors every time we lay the compass. So they are an integral part of the compass. They define the shape and the texture of the crafting we do, and they're largely responsible for channeling the energies for us. We do everything indirectly through the ancestors to a certain extent. And of course the River of Blood, the current of the Tradition is made up from the memories and the energies of our ancestors.

Of course, an obvious way that we use our ancestral connections is in the technique of tapping the bone, or rather the series of techniques that come under the heading of tapping the bone. Tapping the bone is literally getting information from the ancestors, and trying to awaken some of those memories that lie dormant in our genes, in our cellular structure, in our blood and bone if you like.

There are several techniques for doing this, starting with working literally with a piece of human bone, which is probably not as popular today as it used to be in olden times when cunning crafters would carry a human knuckle bone as a pendant around their necks to use for meditating. They would even scrape some pieces of it into their tea to promote vision quests and such like. But nowadays, there's all sorts of reasons why we probably wouldn't do that. However, the metaphorical link, the link that we have with the bone of our ancestors though symbols rather than literal bone can be just as strong. We will obviously work with the skull upon our altar predominantly for this sort of thing. And tapping the bone can literally be taking the wand and tapping on the top of a skull as part of a working. We often tap it on the altar or table three times. And we tend to work with the skull by enfleshing it. We breathe life force into it, and call in one or more particular ancestors to work with.

We may not actually get the lore or whatever it is we're after directly from them, but they act as a herald if you like or a guide, a doorman bringing whatever is necessary so that we can do what we need to do. That may take the form of calling upon the energy of the ancestors to assist us in a working or calling upon the memories, the ancestral memories themselves to try and recover some lore on how to do something in a particular way, which is actually a lot of fun, although it can be a little daunting because you have to really let go of the concept of making a fool of yourself, because you never know where it's going to take you when you do that sort of working.

Recovering the lore is very important. Obviously, despite many grand claims to the contrary, you're not going to find an unbroken chain of Pagan practice stretching back from the modern day right through to pre-Christian Britain. You may find fragments here and there. You may find families that have kept some sort of esoteric practice going without really calling it Pagan or being Pagan in any way. And that's fine, that's cool, as long as it doesn't get misrepresented as being grander than it is. But you can take these pieces, these fragments that you can find out from research and from reading and studying, from talking to people, from working with people who've done that sort of thing, and picking up some hints and tips from them. And then you can take that to the ancestors themselves and work on filling in the gaps, recovering the lost lore, which is what a lot of people do.

We tend to reconstruct our traditions rather than inherit them these days. That doesn't make them any less valid. And it certainly doesn't make them any less potent, but acknowledging that fact does make them a lot more honest. I think that's a very important thing. Even where you do have somebody who has any sort of valid claim of stuff being handed down through generations however long, even they are generally in the situation where they are going to be recovering lore through tapping the bone in some way or another.

One of the really interesting things is that of course in ritual space the aim is to step outside of time for a while. When you're not in the mundane realm, you're really in the eternal now where past, present, and future meet. And so, one of the concepts that people find a little difficult to grasp, but it actually makes perfect sense when you think about it, although most people try not to, is that the ancestors aren't just the people who are from the past. We often refer to our ancestors as "ancestors past, and ancestors yet to be".

Those who come after us are also our ancestors. It helps to not be thinking in too linear a fashion when you start talking about stuff like that. Luckily when we're in the middle of one our rituals, being linear is generally the hardest thing to do. And so you can actually fall into that eternal nowness, the eternal state of becoming, which is so potent and powerful when it comes to working any sort of magic. Of course, in any talk about ancestors, you really can't leave out the oldest of ancestors. Many shamanic traditions and the traditional crafting traditions of the British Isles are no exception here, think of the Gods themselves as being the most ancient ancestors. They see us humans as being part of that continuous line between the gods and modern man. And that's why we always consider that we're all sacred and we all have a divine spark within us. After all, there has to be something of worth within us. Otherwise, why would the ancestors talk to us? Anyway, that's it for today. I hope you enjoyed this. And I hope you'll tune in for future editions of the Crooked Path.

Spring Equinox
Episode 5, broadcast March 20, 2006

Hello, and welcome to the Crooked Path. My name is Peter Paddon and today I'm going to be talking about Spring Equinox. As it's just coming up, literally looming on the horizon, just a day or so away - possibly just a day or so gone past by the time you listen to this - but as I speak right now, it's still ahead of us, just barely.

So, what is Spring Equinox, also known as the vernal equinox, which is the Latin word for spring - vernal that is, not equinox. In the northern hemisphere it's when the sun crosses the celestial equator whilst heading north. And the same event is the autumn equinox for the southern hemisphere. So if you're Australian, you're probably in the middle of celebrating your autumn equinox.

It is the first day of spring in London and the first day of fall in Sydney, is one way of looking at it. But either way, day and night are exactly twelve hours long. Hence, equinox, which means "equal night". It is supposed to be an event, a celestial event that turns men to more lustful thoughts, not that most men ever stop thinking lustful thoughts, at least I certainly don't. But perhaps, I shouldn't think of myself as representative of them, since I'm strange and British.

Anyway, here's some interesting facts about spring and the spring equinox, just to get you going, and then in the second part we'll actually look at spring equinox as it's related to Traditional Witchcraft.

So fun facts, today on the Chinese calendar is considered the midpoint of spring and it's called Chung Fen. They get their spring a little earlier than us, apparently on February the fourth. And in Japan, vernal equinox day is a national holiday. It's a very big day for family reunions. And I guess that's because graduation is this time of year as well. So it's a chance for everyone to get back together after that. In Iran, the vernal equinox is new years day, or NoRuz. The observation of NoRuz in Iran was brought to Islam from Zoroastrianism. That's the religion of the Persian magi, for those that are into biblical links, probably not many people listening to this, maybe one of the three people that listen.

There's a wide spread belief, apparently, that on the equinox it's possible to balance an egg on its end. Sometimes you can, sometimes you can't. Actually, the real thing that makes it possible is where the yolk is in the egg. If the yolk is just right you can actually balance an egg on its end. But the fact that it's equinox doesn't make the odds any better of you succeeding. It's pretty much a shot in the dark anyway.

Now apparently New Hampshire has an American Stonehenge, which I've never heard of before. But it's four thousand years old and is considered by some to be the oldest man made construction in the United States. The sun rises over one monolith and sets over another on the equinoxes. Now I'm going to have to find out where it is and go and visit it, because that's got my interest. And perhaps the most interesting piece of useless information from my perspective is that the spring equinox sets off the Welsh pagan Sabbat of Gwyl Canol or GwenWynol which is more commonly known as Eostre or Ostara, and in the Mabinogion, it's the day on which the restored Llew takes his vengeance on Goronwy by piercing him with the sunlight spear, which is a particularly favorite story of mine, because Llew is my patron. So we'll be talking about that a little bit more later. I hope you enjoyed the fun facts, next up we'll be talking about traditional witchcraft and the equinox.

So, let's talk about spring equinox in Traditional Witchcraft, the Cunning Arts, the Elder Faith, whatever you want to call it. Way back in the day when I used to be a high priest of an Alexandrian coven back in England, the equinoxes always posed a bit of a problem for us, because we never really knew what to do with them.

26

We ended up actually using the equinoxes as occasions when we would have guests who might be interested in coming along and training with us. That worked out quite well, but it didn't really give us any great insights, and we probably could have made a lot better use of our time than just having a sort of open day. But there you go.

In Traditional Witchcraft, first of all, you're much less likely to have invited guests to a Traditional Witchcraft rite, because it's just not really a done thing. You tend to be working in your rites, and you don't want to be side-tracked by having to look after people who don't know what's going on. And for the same reason, we tend not to do public rituals either. We have done public rituals in the past, but it's become something that we don't do anymore, because we want to focus on actually doing the work for us and for our tradition.

And so, the main thing that we have with spring equinox is that you have to take into account the fact that we work a mystery cycle. We don't work an agricultural cycle. Wicca and a lot of the more popular Pagan ways of doing things tend to work on the folk practices of everyday people. And so, the Sabbats tend to be tied up with agriculture, with what's going on in farms, with the animals and the crops. And that's why they tend to be tied up with fertility and stuff like that. We work a Sacred King cycle, which is quite different. It's more to do with the growth and mental fertility, if you like, of the individual initiate. And so, we work things in quite a different way. But we often nod our head in the direction of the agricultural cycle just because it can be fun - certainly on Beltain, we get into the whole earthy nature of that rite, although even then we're looking at a different aspect of it.

For us, the spring equinox is very much a time of individual work. The other festivals tend to be more group oriented, but both of the equinoxes, both spring and fall, are very much catering to the path of the individual, and are very closely tied into whole concept of the path of the outcast, that you may remember that I talked about way back in the pilot episode of this podcast. The way we deal with the Sacred King cycle could be the way it is often practiced in traditional groups, by appointing somebody Sacred King for the year. They represent the group going around the wheel of the year doing the various things.

We used to do that, but we've actually moved into a mode of operation where everybody in the group is walking the Wheel as Sacred King for themselves. And it's actually working very well for us, because what we get is everybody gets the insights that previously only the person carrying the Sacred King was getting, so we really like it that way. But it does tend to accentuate the effects of the Sabbats, all of them, on our members.

So we become very intimately aware of what's going on, which is a good thing, but it's a mixed blessing as well, because it means you also suffer all the negative sides rather intensely as well. But that's part of life. You suffer to learn and you learn to suffer, I guess. So the Sacred King cycle, equinox is probably best expressed through the myth of Lleu Llaw Gyffes, the Welsh god of light, and incidentally my personal patron. And although as I said before, the Welsh Pagan Sabbat is often seen as being about the revenge of Llew on Goronwy. And it is to a certain extent, and we'll talk about that in a little bit. But the main slant of it for us and my particular group is the part of the myth of Llew where he's working through the prohibition that was that placed on him by his mother Arianrhod. In the beginning she told him that he would have no name unless she gave it to him, and she would never name him.

Gwydion helped Llew to trick her into giving him a name. And that's how he became Lleu Llaw Gyffes… Llew managed to win his name from his mother, Lleu Llaw Gyffes. Then she set out her second curse which was that he would never receive arms unless she gave them to him and she would never do that. And so, once again Gwydion helped out. He disguised the two of them as bards. And they arrived at Arianrhod's castle one evening. And in those days, it was traditional to always extend hospitality to traveling bards, so you basically gave them bed and board in exchange for a couple of songs, because that was how news got about in those days.

In the middle of the night, Gwideon made it seem that the castle was being attacked, and Arianrhod and her handmaidens came out and asked them to help defend the castle, because all the men folk were already away fighting a battle somewhere else. She handed them weapons and armor and got her handmaidens to dress Gwydion in the armor while she put the armor on the young lad, whereupon Gwydion started taking his armor off saying "Ok, It's all done now. You've given him arms." And she goes "Damn it, curse it, curse it." That's when she says that he'll never have a wife who's of mortal birth. That's a whole other story, so I'm not going to take time going over that just yet. But, the whole thing of naming and arming is what comes in for us at the spring equinox, because it is the coming of age part of the cycle.

The Sacred King cycle is very simple. Well, I would say that. I've been walking it for a couple of years now. We start at Imbolc where the lord is brought forth as the child of promise from the cauldron by the maiden. It's not a birth. It's a little more complicated than that. It's a coming into manifestation. His birth was actually earlier. And I'll explain that in a second, but bear with me. So he's brought forth as the child of promise at Imbolc, and then at spring equinox is his coming of age. And that's the whole point of the naming and arming, because in Celtic society for a boy to become a man he had to receive his arms. He had to be be-weaponed, as it were. And so the whole thing about it is that he takes his arms and becomes an adult in the eyes of his contemporaries.

The way we see it is that at that point he then goes off to seek his fortune. And we call that the exile, which lasts right through until autumn equinox, when he comes back to serve as Priest-King for the tribal clan, or whatever you want to call it. It's very complex.

Of course, in the Sabbats in between there are various things that go on which probably as we come to them, I will do a podcast about, just to keep you interested.

So that's basically the key thing. The naming and arming of Llew is very important to us, because obviously his name has a lot of significance. And arming is - for us it's more of a giving you the skills or giving you the ability to acquire the skills that you need to follow your path rather than actual physical weapons, and it can be very intense.

There's quite a few years where the outcome has been a very huge sense of "fuck you", which has not gone down well. But we've actually managed to find a way to explore the same mystery without going to quite that extreme, and things have been running a little smoother ever since we did that. Actually part of that process was taking the Sacred King concept and, instead of embedding it one person, letting everybody partake of it. It's seems to come in a lot more saner that way.

Of course, the story in the first part where I mentioned the revenge of Llew, where he takes his vengeance on Goronwy, basically at the point where Llew is killed in the legend, he's standing with one foot in the caldron and one foot on the goat's back under the roof with no walls, and he get's pierced with a spear that's been made in a year of Sundays by Goronwy. He's actually facing in a particular direction.

The positioning, when you look at the Celtic constellations and what represents the cauldron, the goat, and all the rest of it, it basically gives you the positioning of autumn equinox, and the idea is that when Llew had his revenge on Goronwy, he made him stand in the same position, but facing the other way, which of course would be spring equinox. And that why it's associated with that. So, to a lesser extent, we look at that as well, because many people, many traditions follow the concept of the lord of darkness and the lord of light, or oak king, holly king, stuff like that. And we don't really do that in any serious way in our tradition. But we do acknowledge that there is a sort of, an exchange going on. We do it at the equinoxes.

A lot of people do it at the solstices, but it's historically the Celts seemed to have preferred the equinoxes for that. And it works better that way for us, so that's what we do. Because we use Llew and Goronwy as our lord of darkness and lord of light, it seems a fairly obvious choice. Our line demarking the dark half of the year from the light half of the year goes from equinox to equinox. And it coincidently, that's also the path of the initiate, the path of the exile. And it works really well for us. So that's pretty much it.

That's all I've got to say today. And I hope you liked it. Please remember, if you like what I'm doing to vote every month at podcastalley and podcastpickle to help us get a little better known. And don't forget that the web site, crookedpath.org, also has a complete forum where you can let us know what you think. You can suggest ideas for topics to discuss and generally interact with us in a meaningful way. And there's also articles and stuff, not many at the moment. But I plan to have more as time goes by. So please feel free to explore crookedpath.org and sign up and have an account there, so that maybe we can to know each other a little better. Anyway, hope you enjoyed it.

Witch's Mark and Witch Blood

Episode 7, broadcast April 3, 2006

Hello, and welcome to the Crooked Path. My name is Peter Paddon. And today, we're going to take a look at the concept of Witch Blood. But first, let's talk about the fabled Witch's Mark.

The Witch Mark is an interesting concept. It has existed for a very long time in literature and mythology, and a lot of interesting things have been said about it over the years. In literature, you often find the idea of the Witch's Mark being an extra nipple or teat often under the armpit that is used to feed your familiar or an imp or devil given to you by Satan.

Obviously, Witches are not really Satanic, so that really doesn't apply here. Witch Marks are also seen as, in some stories, as brand marks or marks of possession, like cattle brands, or natural deformities or blemishes on the skin, which show that you have the Witch's birth-right if you like. There's a whole range of things really, though most of it stems from the time of the Inquisition, when there was quite a trade in Witch-finding.

Matthew Hopkins, a famous Witch finder of England, the Witch-Finder General, and quite a large number of fellows of a similar nature, used to go around charging a penny a time - or in some cases a shilling a time - to identify Witches. They would do this by looking for the Witch's Mark.

According to the Inquisition, the Witch Mark was a mark that was placed on the body by Satan himself at the Witch's initiation, and it was frequently described as being a suckling place for the familiar or imp. But it was usually seen as a discoloration of some sort, or at least it started out that way, that was impervious to pain.

The way they used to search for it was by sticking pins in you. They had a particular type, a pin called a bodkin, which was a long sharp pin with a wooden handle. They would prod away at you until they found a somewhere that you didn't feel any pain.

That's all well and good, except that you have to remember the fact that there are areas in the human body where the skin doesn't have that many pain receptors. So you can find points where you can stick a pin in without causing pain, even in a perfectly normal person. There are also lots of reasons why areas of insensitivity might arise, due to injury or illness, so there was plenty of opportunity for them to find what would be considered at the time as real Witch's Marks.

But you have to remember these guys were earning a living with this, and so they tended to hedge their bets a little. They would have trick bodkins, ones where they were able to allow the pin to retract into the handle to give the appearance of piercing the skin without causing any pain. As time went by, this became a very common practice. It was a good way to earn a living in those times, and there were always plenty of people willing to have a go.

So as you would expect, there were people being accused left, right, and center during the time of the Inquisition. And the strangest things became referred to as Witch's Marks. There are actually some historical ones that are long standing. For example, the possession of an extra finger on one hand was seen as the mark of the Witch. Ann Boleyn was said to have six fingers on her left hand. And the left hand is of course significant here. And though she was never actually openly accused of Witchcraft, if I remember rightly, mainly because she was married to the king at the time, but certainly when she had her head removed from her shoulders, part of the reason was because she was considered to be a Witch.

But as time went by, pretty much any deformity or irregularity of the body could be referred to as a Witch's Mark, if the bearer of

34

the unfortunate stigmata happens to have land that somebody else wanted or had somehow upset or annoyed somebody in some way. So pretty much anything could be considered the Witch's Mark at that point. It was all fair game for the sticking of fake pins into the body, and ending up at the gallows or on the bon fire if you were really unlucky.

So is there any significance to the Witch's Mark? Is there any basis in fact on it? Well, that really depends on who you talk to. Most Witches will say that there is not a physical mark that is placed on the body, but there is a spiritual mark that happens during your initiation, whether it be a spontaneous initiation that happens within, or the rite of passage into a coven or group. There is said to be a mark placed on your aura that all other Witches can see.

There is certainly something about someone who has undergone a true initiation. You certainly get a feeling that they might be "one of us" as it were. And so I'm inclined to believe it.

There are some traditions do practice more or less temporary markings in tandem with initiation. They may mark the Mark of Cain, which is of course another classic example of the Witch's Mark: a circle-cross or a crow's foot or goose foot somewhere on the body. Usually it is marked temporarily, but there are traditions that still do it permanently. In the old days, it would have been marked with a Blackthorn thorn - try saying that ten times fast - because the Blackthorn has rather a lot of bacteria on the thorn, and it was necessary to make use of what you'd learned by way of wort cunning, or herb lore, to prevent sickness or even death as a result from having your skin scratched by the very sharp Blackthorn. And it would always leave a scar. And that was really quite an effective way of doing it.

Nowadays, there are other ways to test herb lore skills, and so I doubt there's many groups, if any at all, who actually scratch you with a Blackthorn anymore. But there are other ways of marking, with the number of different groups and different traditions that are out there, pretty much every part of the spectrum is covered somewhere I would imagine.

So the Witch Mark, yes it does exist, has existed historically as a physical mark. Nowadays, it's more likely to be a metaphysical marking in the aura. Hollywood and the Spanish Inquisition made full use of it, took poetic license to the extreme and made it into something quite spectacular. And that's the Witch's Mark for you.

So there's been a lot of fuss lately in the Pagan chat rooms, forums and email lists, or what have you, about Witch Blood, the idea of whether a Witch is born or made. And there's a lot of people, especially younger solitary people, who are promoting the idea that they were born a Witch, and that they have the Witch Blood and that's the only real way to become a Witch.

Meanwhile, there are other people who are arguing that the only way to become a Witch is to train and initiate with a group. There's a lot of politics, and a lot of personal opinion, and a lot of bile, quite frankly, being exchanged from person to person, not in a good way I hasten to add, about this whole concept of Witch Blood.

It has been used in the past in arguments for and against traditional hereditary family trads. And bad blood, if you'll pardon the expression, was also evident in those arguments. Although they seem to have died down lately, nobody really has a claim to be famtrad anymore. It's just not the done thing. Even the people who consider themselves to be famtrad don't make public claims of that sort anymore.

But what exactly is Witch Blood? And why is there so much fuss about it? Well, part of the problem is that Witch Blood has made its way into literature, into fiction and television shows like the series Charmed. The idea that the "Charmed Ones" were born a special way, have this special DNA that is instilled in them at birth that makes them able to be the "Charmed Ones". Mere ordinary Wiccans cannot hope to become "Charmed Ones", or part of their coven, because they weren't born Witches. And this has entered into the fantasy life of people who would like to think they're Witches. Serious Witches tend not to make such a big deal about it, but there are a bunch of people out there who basically use the Witch-born idea as an excuse for why they don't have to read any books, or do any studying, or actually do any practical work at all. It's really quite sad.

I'm not speaking about everybody there, though. Everybody knows at least one person who's like that, who makes all the claims and backs it up with absolutely nothing, and this is a common theme where Witch Blood is concerned. However Witch Blood, like the Witch Mark has been around a lot longer than the modern Pagan online community. In fact, you could trace it back as far as the Sumerian and Babylonian myths with the Anunaki, and Enki and Enlil creating humanity.

Then there was Lilith and Lilitu and what eventually became the story of Adam and Eve in the Christian Bible - there really is quite interesting material in those myths, when you read that the first man was created, and then his children, his first children were actually not sired by Adamu - the first man - but were rather sired by Enki upon the lady who became Eve, or in other versions of the story on Lilith.

These, the offspring of this union with Enki ended up being the Witch Blood, the Watchers - there's lots of different names for them, the overseers, even the vampires. In some stories they end up becoming the vampires of myth and lore. But whatever else you can say, there certainly seems to be a trend that was started by the Sumerians and the Babylonians. Another version of the Witch Blood story starts with Tiamat, the mother of dragons. And dragon blood is a very important metaphor for Witch Blood.

Of course, in Semitic realms, and in fact throughout Europe, it ended up that the Witches were the Children of Cain. Cain was marked because of killing his brother and he went off to the Land of Nod and lived with the non-Edenic people, and they ended up being the ancestors of modern Witches, so the storey goes, including the grandson of Cain, who was Tubal Cain, the first blacksmith.

Because of this, there's a lot of blacksmith lore tied up in Traditional Witchcraft. It's actually a very interesting thing to study, but it'll suck you in there. You'll be reading books, and perusing web sites, and visiting museums for years. Chasing this down is a fascinating subject.

Anyway further down the line, the Witch Blood, the divine blood if you like, makes its way into the Merovingian court, the Dragon Kings of Europe, who claimed Fairy origins, as well as the whole Holy Blood, Holy Grail thing with Mary Magdalene. I'm not going to bore you with the details of that. Just wait till the movie comes out, "The Da Vinci Code". And they'll fill you in with all the details. And I'll leave it up to you to believe what you want to believe.

I'm actually quite fond of the theory of JC and Mary Magdalene getting together and producing a sprog, but that's because I'm strange, and things like that tickle my fancy. But we'll move swiftly on from that. The basic idea is that there is this strand of DNA, if you like, this genetic marker that makes you a Witch or doesn't. And most people would say bullpucky, because nine times out of ten there's a... it's being implied that I am the one who has this and you don't. And so it's used in a very elitist way, a very silly way, by all arguments.

There is also the fact that if you go back far enough in time any DNA strand that was exclusive to one particular family will by now have been diluted through the entire human population. So

38

chances are more likely than not that I have this Witch Blood DNA, and you have this Witch Blood DNA, and the person sitting next to you at work has this Witch Blood DNA, which is really quite depressing. Of course, theories have a habit of evolving, and I'm actually quite in favor of this.

I like the idea of there being this divine spark in our genetic make-up. And what the current way of looking at it is, is that we all have this spark, we all have the potential if you like. But the potential has to be awakened and that's easier to do in some people than in others. Just like recessive genes for hair color and eye color come and go and skip generations, so does the propensity to activate this particular genetic marker if you like, and wake up the Witch Blood.

Generally, you're looking at an experience like a life threatening experience, a traumatic experience or a carefully constructed initiatory experience within a training group to do this awakening. Or sometimes it can be spontaneous in those that are gifted or cursed, depending on your perspective. Basically, the idea is that, as Robert Cochran said - and has been quoted frequently by many people - "A Witch is born not made". Well, this is only half of the story. The full quote should be, "A Witch is born not made. But if a Witch is to be made, then tears must be shed beneath the moon light" or something like that.

Basically the idea is that you have to be both born, you have the nature inclination and propensity towards Witchcraft, but then that has to be triggered, it has to be woken up. You have to awaken the ancestral memories, and this is what the training and education within a coven or working group is all about.

That's one of the reasons why Traditional Witches tend to want to pass stuff on, because part of the process is awakening. Certainly in the group I'm in, we do a lot of work trying to recover lore through ancestral memory, which is really quite another subject, and we'll probably have a podcast on that at some point in the future. But for now, we're done with Witch Blood.

So, I hope you enjoyed it, and I hope it's given you some food for thought.

Witch-Wear & Herb Lore
Episode 9, broadcast April 17, 2006

Hi, this is Peter Paddon and you're listening to the Crooked Path. Today, I'm going to take a look at herb lore, but first let's talk about what Witches wear.

There are of course a lot of stereotypes of Witches' appearances, coming from all periods of history. Obviously the most familiar stereotype of the Witch is the black garbed, pointy hatted, green faced hag riding a broom stick that we all know and love from Halloween festivals across the world.

But there is actually a modern stereotype that seems to be forming itself quite nicely, and all you have to do to see it is to go to any public Pagan celebration, especially Sabbats. Certainly, here on the West Coast this is true, and from what I hear, it's pretty much a universal thing. It is the renfair-garb-wearing Pagan.

It can be a little disconcerting. You know, you turn up to do a serious piece of work in a public ritual - or as serious as you can do in a public setting - and there's all these people dressed up in Elizabethan costumes, badly fitting. It can get quite scary sometimes. The level of beauty that you see arrayed before you is very distracting at the very least. It prompted me to decide to talk today about what Witches wear.

What is it that Witches should be wearing whilst they are crafting, whilst doing their rituals? It is a subject that does crop up from time to time, and there can be some quite heated debate. Obviously, the first option is the robe. Traditionally, Witches and magicians wear robes, and this could actually be a really good idea for some people. The basic idea is that you have a set of clothing that you only wear for ritual.

So that means that part of your preparation is taking off the clothing that you wear for your day job or that you've been having a row with your spouse in, or chasing the kids and clipping them around the ear. You put all that to one side, and put on this special set of clothing that is only ever used in ritual sacred space, which helps you to really put on the persona, put on the frame of mind, to enable you to go in and actually do some serious work and leave the mundane world behind for a time.

I think it can actually be very valuable. And this is especially true of ceremonial magic where the symbolism that is built into the regalia is very significant for the working. They can get very precise. I mean, even the shape of the robe itself is symbolic. The classic ceremonial robe is a tau robe. It'll be a hooded robe with long sleeves that flare out a little bit, and basically, when you look at it, it's a tau cross or an ankh with a hood.

This of course is quite a potent universal ancient symbol that denotes life and energy and power and so on and so forth, and the tau cross itself can be seen to be a particular arrangement of the spheres of the tree of life if you're into the Qabala. This can take you a long way into your ritual symbolism before you've even set foot in the temple, and then on top of that, you have the cords, the emblems, the insignia, the lamens , badges, anything else that they wear, all of which is carefully crafted to have very very specific meaning and symbolism, often pertaining to a specific ritual rather than to just to their traditional path.

So you can get very specific, very focused, just from getting dressed, which is kind of cool. Not that many Witches wear robes these days. I have worked with groups that have robes. When I did my initial training in an Alexandrian coven, we were all required to wear robes... sorry, all required to possess robes, robes that we never ever ever wore. But we all had to have them just in case. I guess, it was an emergency measure in case the police raided or something.

But like I said, we never actually wore them. And I'll talk about not wearing robes later on as well.

But there's this whole idea nowadays of people attending public rituals dressed in renfair garb. And I find this frankly a little disturbing, because whilst some of it can be extremely beautiful and of course everyone is entitled to dress up in something special for their Sabbats, there is really a disconcerting concept of making the whole thing a fantasy. If you're wearing renfair garb when you're going playing with the SCA or down at the renfair and then you wear that same garb to ritual, what are you really saying about how you perceive your Paganism and your crafting? Is it really just another fantasy and something that you sort of put on and take away as a form of entertainment?

It really does bother me when I see people in renfair garb for that reason, because frequently they seem to, it seems to be very easy to put on the renfair persona with the renfair garb, where what you really want is the Pagan or Witchly persona. So I really think renfair garb is not a good idea, although I suppose it's never going to go away, so I'm going to have to learn to live with it.

So what should you and should you not wear for serious ritual work? Well, there's a saying that a real Witch can do magic anywhere and in anything. If you can't work stark naked in a concrete bunker with a bath plunger in your hand then you can't do magic at all. And there's something to that. However, what you do or don't wear can go a long way towards helping or hindering your crafting.

On many levels, psychologically, if you associate wearing particular type of clothing with doing ritual, that helps you get into your ritual space that much quicker, because it starts the process going as soon as you start getting changed, like I was talking about before, with ceremonial garb for the magicians. But there's also stuff that can be seen as an impedance to actually doing crafting, though there's not really much that will actually stop your crafting.

If your clothing gets in the way, then you really need to work on improving your technique, that's all I can say. But there are a couple of things you might want to bear in mind for comfort reasons. It's a good idea to wear loose clothing, because you can find yourself doing some rather strange movements in ritual. And you're probably going to be standing for a prolonged period of time, so you don't want to wear restricting clothing that's going to become uncomfortable under those circumstances. You don't want to be dressed in layer after layer of warm clothing when the temple space is going to get very hot, because you're doing a fire working indoors or something like that. You really need to look at the practicalities and make sure your clothing is loose and comfortable for ritual. And beyond that it doesn't really matter then, whatever works.

My coven and myself, we most frequently work in everyday street clothes. We might take our shoes off if we feel the urge, certainly take our watches off. But beyond that, whatever you're wearing during the day is what you wear. We wear a cord, because we have a lot of symbolism to go with the cord. But beyond that we generally wear street clothes. In the summer when our temple gets a little on the warm side, not having air conditioning, we may switch to wearing sarongs, because it's just plain more comfortable. But that's really the only concession.

On very very rare occasions we might wear robes. We all have robes, but generally we don't use them except occasionally for special reasons, and not for sacrifices or stuff like that - though you don't want to get blood on your day clothes. But sometimes it's nice to have everyone dressed in black so that we can sort of blend into the background to help with getting into a particular type of altered state, or for other purely practical reasons like that.

But you certainly won't find us wearing renfair garb, because I would throw a hissy fit if I saw one of my people doing that, because I'm silly like that. Really it's what's practical.

Some groups like to have everyone dress the same for all kinds of psychological and magical reasons. But it really isn't that important. You wear with feels right for you. What you should not be wearing is a whole bunch of assorted Pagan jewelry because if the symbolism is valid, if you've got too much you're just going to end up with a conflict somewhere. And of course, you don't want to be weighed down if you're working a ritual near running water. You might get carried away and drown if you're got too much silver on you, because it might weigh you down.

But generally speaking, just wear what is practical and comfortable for what you're doing. And really don't worry about anything else, unless your tradition stipulates you have to wear a particular garment. There are some that do that. And they will usually have a pretty good explanation why. But generally speaking, working solitary, working with a group that doesn't have any strict clothing requirements then go with what works, essentially.

Some people like to keep a set of clothing specifically for ritual for the same reasons that ceremonial magicians have their special robes. And it doesn't have to be something special. I remember somebody had a pair of white jogging pants that she used to wear for ritual and a white tee shirt, because she liked wearing white. But she wanted something practical, so she could move around. And so, she basically had her sweats in white that she only wore for ritual. And that was cool. Some people maybe want to keep a perfectly ordinary pair set of day clothes, but ones that they only wear for ritual. Once again, that's fine too.

Of course, the big question is all about wearing no clothes at all. I mentioned the idea of crafting while standing naked in a concrete bunker earlier. And there are a lot of groups, the Gardnerians like to work skyclad. Some of the Alexandrians do, while there are not as many as the Gardnerians in Wicca. And there are some traditional Witchcraft groups that also work skyclad - and there are a lot that don't.

Most traditional Witchcraft groups do not work skyclad, generally speaking. And that's got nothing to do with the old argument of how northern Europeans would not be going out in the snow naked. Because, no they wouldn't go out in the snow naked but they might work naked indoors with a roaring fire. So, you can't really generalize like that. For example, my own group, although we work clothed 99.9% of the time, we are always clothing optional. And we do sometimes have somebody in the circle who feels the need to not be encumbered by clothing, especially if they're carrying an aspect of some sort, centering the circle. Sometimes you just feel there's a need to remove all barriers and so you do. And I don't think it's really giving away anything to say that we always work our initiation rituals skyclad. It's a tradition that we follow and we find very useful. For the rest of the time, jeans and tee shirt. It's really quite simple.

So as far as I'm concerned, once again unless your tradition has specific guidance on the matter, skyclad or not should be down to your personal choice. And actually when you do skyclad, for those of you that haven't tried skyclad, it's actually a lot less titillating and a lot less troublesome than you might imagine. You get busy in the ritual and you pretty much forget about being skyclad, especially if everyone else is skyclad. It then actually becomes interesting when somebody comes in who is robed, because you find yourself watching the robed person and ignoring the naked people. That's human nature, I guess. You always look for what's different. So anyway, what do Witches wear? Whatever they damn well please, is the short answer. So that's that.

And now on to herb lore or wortcunning. I should warn you I'm about to have a little bit of a rant here, because if there's one thing that really drives me crazy it's the absolute crap that you can find about herb lore online. Please, please, do not take anything as gospel that you read on line about herb lore. I have read some of the most atrocious drivel that's supposed to be herb lore.

And the really scary thing is that a lot of the stuff that is really bad is medical herb lore. The last thing in the world you want to make a mess up on is medical herb lore. So please, use reliable sources when you're researching anything to do with herbs, whether it's for magical, medical, or beautician purposes. Just make sure that your source is reliable. Don't pay any attention to some of the wild-ass crap that you'll find on line. Some people are so irresponsible with their web sites, it really really concerns me.

On that subject, let's talk a little bit about healing herbs. Now, I am not going to recommend any herbs for medical conditions, and I heartily recommend that you do the same - Ok? The important thing to remember here is that if you diagnose or treat illness when you are not a medical qualified practitioner, there's two things that you're leaving yourself wide open to. Number one, is you're leaving yourself wide open to be sued by the person that you're advising, because you're not qualified to give them that advice. If it turns out to be not beneficial to them, guess what? They can sue your ass.

The other thing you're also leaving yourself wide open to is some time in jail, because guess what - it is an offense to impersonate a medical practitioner. And that's what you're doing. You're playing doctor. So don't do it, unless you have a medical qualification, do not diagnose or treat any illnesses from anybody. Now you may be a member of a coven or group where they say otherwise. Well, that's between you and your coven. I don't want to know.

But I'm saying, my advice to you is if you want to play around with the medical use of herbs, practice on yourself, because you're not likely to sue yourself. And they're not likely to arrest you for practicing on yourself either. Otherwise, we'd all be in trouble. So should you want to look into healing herbs for your own personal use, remember, don't go by some of the crap that's out there on the internet.

My suggestion is to stick to a good reliable source such as "A Modern Herbal" by Grieve. It's pretty much the best of the herbal books, and it's pretty cheap as well, if you buy it on Amazon or at your local metaphysical book store. You should always support your local Pagan businesses, of course.

"A Modern Herbal" by Mrs. Grieve is really really a very very good book, and I heartily recommend also getting a book called "A Herbal Medicine Maker's Handbook" by Green, which has a little bit of the medical herb lore in it, but more importantly, it tells you what to do with the herbs, how to make your teas, your poultices, your creams, lotions, etc., out of the herbs once you've decided what you want to use. It's a really good book. It's a lot of fun, and it tells you how to do everything with everyday bits and pieces you'll find in the kitchen rather than buying expensive laboratory equipment. Not quite as efficient, but a damn sight cheaper and a lot of fun as well.

I use a cream that I make myself for eczema on my hands. It's a recipe that my brother gave me. He is a qualified medical practitioner, and he teaches naturopathy, aromatherapy, reflexology, and acupuncture in Canada. His name is Colin Paddon if you ever come across him, in Ontario. He's really good at what he does. And he's a great healer as well. Just a little plug for my brother, in case he's listening. But the lotion that I make, I use the herbs that he told me to use, and I make them up using the recipe that's in the "Herbal Medicine Maker's Handbook". It is brilliant, a really nice moisturizing cream basically, that works wonders for my cracked skin.

So check out those two books if you want to do the herbal medicine route. And obviously the best way to do that is to actually

48

go get qualified as a medical herbal practitioner. Courses are very expensive, and they're difficult to find. But there are some really good ones out there. So, it's worth the trouble if that's what you're interested in.

Of course, if you're like me, your interest in herbs is more likely to be involved in using them magically. And there are a couple of different way you can do that. You can use them in incense, of course, and you can also use them in mojo bags, and other nefarious and interesting ways. We're going to talk a little bit about a few of those.

I'm not going to be too specific because the herbs you use magically tend to be down to correspondences for the tradition that you follow, and obviously, you might not follow the same sort of tradition that I do, so any correspondences I give you may not be particularly useful. Most tables of correspondences tend to work on a planetary setting, so that's a good place to start. But you may work Qabalisticly, in which case the spheres of the Tree of Life would be your focal point. Or you may work in some other system completely.

The important thing is that you have a table of correspondences where this herb corresponds with that event or that energy, and so on and so forth that deity, and that will help you decide what herbs to use magically.

Using them in incense is pretty straight forward - you make an interesting blend. One of the things that often gets left out when people are making their own incense, try and work with the quantities that you're using in such a way that you end up with something that not going to make you cough and choke in the middle of your ritual. Something that smells half way decent is always a good idea.

There's actually a really simple way of working this. The trick here is that you start off by having a bowl with some coffee grounds in by your side. What you do is you take the ingredients that you've decided need to go into this incense, and you start off by getting an idea of what they smell like individually by having a charcoal block burning, and you put a little bit, and it really has to be a little bit, you don't pile the stuff on - I mean literally just a pinch - and hold your nose over it and waft into your nostrils and see what it smells like.

In between each ingredient, what you should do is take a good sniff of the coffee grounds, because that clears your nasal palate so you don't get any left over from the previous scent while you're smelling the current scent. It's a little trick from the fragrance industry which somebody once shared with me, and it really does work well.

Once you've familiarized yourself with the scent of each individual ingredient, you then want to decide what your main ingredient is going to be and then start experimenting. The trick here is to play with different quantities. Don't just put an equal amount of each in and expect it's going to smell lovely. For example, if you're doing a horned god incense, you might want to start of with oak moss because it's got that nice rich earthy forest smell to it, and it's really really quite strong. That might be half of your recipe, just the oak moss, and then you might want to put something in.

You've got earthy and mossy and foresty there, but you want to sweeten it up a little bit. So maybe a little tiny bit mistletoe oil added to the oak moss would be really cool, and in that way you just sort of tweak things until you get a scent that's really pleasing, and really says to you what it is you want the incense to be used for.

The other trick is to try and have at least one of the ingredients as an oil, as an essential oil. The reason for this is that it'll make sure it burns more smoothly, and you'll also get a lot more smoke from the incense, which of course is the point of burning incense - to get nice wafts of smoke that smell pretty, drifting around in the temple. So at least one ingredient as an oil is usually a pretty good idea. Also, try not to over-do the resin. Resin is really cool stuff, but if you have too many resins in your recipe, you end up with a sticky mess on your charcoal, which doesn't work at all. So, you want have something that is herb, that is leaf or wood or stem and use that as a base, and then have some resin, some oil and then work on from there.

What you get then, is that there is a nice incense because you've balanced scents together. It smells good. It evokes the energies of what it is that you want to use it for, and you've also got a good texture thing going which gives you different types of smoke, so it tends to burn for longer and smoke for longer as well. You end up with a very well-crafted incense, and people will be absolutely amazed. So that's the secret tips to incense making.

To make a Mojo bag? You use exactly the same herbs, but you throw them in a cotton bag to use as a sort of herbal talisman. You might throw a few semi-precious stones in there, obviously sticking to the correspondences again, and away you go. So it's really quite simple. I'm not going to dwell on that one too much.

Another way of using herbal ingredients magically is - this might sound really silly, but - dressing your altar. There's an old ritual I use occasionally for consecrating a magical ring. It's from the Greek Magical Papyri, so it's a couple of thousand years old now. One of the things it does, it uses laurel leaves to dress the altar. You basically have your bowl of oil that you're going to use to consecrate that ring, and you surround it with laurel leaves. It's basically symbolic value there. And you can do stuff like that with dressing your altar, dressing your shrine, dressing the temple for that matter.

Making a wreath to hang behind your altar for the Sabbat is a nice way of using herbs in a magical way. So you know, ingenuity and imagination is the key here. Stick with your correspondences. Stick with what your tradition says is appropriate for the season or for the working and away you go. It's as simple as that.

Then of course there is one of the areas of use of herbal lore in magic that has be approached rather carefully and that is herbs and trance states. It is possible to give your trance states a boost and remain total legal. I know the wonders of hashish are well documented, but there's actually stuff that is much better to use magically, mainly because it doesn't end up invoking jail cells around you.

Perhaps the most commonly used trance inducing herb you'll find is mugwort. Mugwort is really good. You can put a little bit into your incense and it becomes a dream inducing or astral projection inducing or path working incense extraordinaire. The trick is to not over do it. Too much mugwort is going to leave you feeling very stupid. And you can get psychologically hooked on it as well. So use it sparingly. You don't want to sort of throw a fist full of mugwort on the charcoal block and just stick your head over it. That would not be a good thing. So mugwort I can heartily recommend, but you have to take it a little carefully. Use it in moderation, like all things, and you'll find it will enhance your trance work, it'll enhance path workings, journey work, anything of that nature. Also, oracular work, divination, it's very good for that.

For visionary stuff, if you use it properly salvia divinorum[1] is very good, also known as diviner's sage. You can actually get that from a lot of places. The best thing to do is find somebody who can give or sell you a plant and grow your own, because that way you can guarantee the purity.

---

1   NOTE: Salvia Divinorum has been made illegal in several states. Check to make sure it is legal where you live.

One of the really cool things about salvia divinorum is that it is, they haven't found a toxic level for it yet. You can ingest a wheel barrow load of the stuff without any harm. They reckon that if there is a toxic level, you're going to fall asleep in a stupor before you'll hit the point where it's actually starting to do you any harm.

Now, taking salvia divinorum the traditional way is little tricky because it involves wedging a huge amount of leaf into your mouth, chewing it and letting the saliva and juice gather under your tongue. It's really unpleasant, it's really bitter. Some people might like it, I personally can't stand it.

You can buy salvia leaves that have been treated with a concentrated extract. I'm not really into that. It's not really the natural approach. You can also smoke it. My favorite way of using it is you can get these vaporizers that are actually sold for people who are using medical marijuana. It is like a little pipe, and has a little burning plate. You can finely chop your salvia and vaporize it on the plate, and that actually works incredibly well. It's a lot healthier than smoking it in a roll up, because you usually have to cut it with tobacco to make that work. So you're avoiding the tobacco.

You're actually avoiding hot smoke which can do damage to the tissue of your lungs, because the vaporized leaf, the vapor that you actually inhale, is only slightly warmer than room temperature by the time you inhale it. So it actually is a lot healthier for you. So if you're going to do it, do it that way. The other option is doing it the old fashioned way, the bitter leaf under the tongue. And you have to sort of keep it there for about fifteen minutes, chewing every now and then, trying not to drool green liquid everywhere. It can be messy. So that's salvia divinorum.

Perhaps my all time favorite is wormwood, which is a little tricky to use. Basically, what you want to do with wormwood is you want to take absinthe. Now there's a slight problem with absinthe in that it is not legal to make or sell absinthe in this country[2], although you can import it from over seas if you do so quietly. They don't like you bringing it in in large quantities, but you can buy a bottle of it from London and such places.

You can actually do a better job in most cases if you make your own. Obviously, you can't distill your own absinthe, but you can get a reasonable approximation. If you get a decent vodka and some good quality wormwood[3] as well - once again it's best to grow your own, but you can buy dried wormwood if that's all you can get your hands on. The fresh stuff is so much better though, believe me. If you get one of the larger bottles of Smirnoff vodka, blue label is stronger than red label remember. And the stronger it is, the better it's going to work.

You basically take a small fist-full of wormwood and about an equal quantity of mint or lemon balm, and if you can throw some star anise in as well, that really helps. And what you do is you leave it in the bottle. You should probably transfer it into a mason jar so you've got the wide neck, it makes life a little easier. You put a fist-full of mint, a fist-full of wormwood, and maybe half a dozen star anise capsules, you know those little star shaped things into the big bottle's worth of vodka and give it a good shake at least once a day. And leave that for seven or eight days. And then you're good to go. You strain out all the herby bits, and you should have a nice green liquid at this point.

If you were allowed to legally distill it, you would then distill that, and then take a second bunch of mint leaves and wormwood and steep that in the distilled liquid for another seven days and then strain it again. That would be real absinthe. But without the distillation, you can get a perfectly useable beautiful green liquid that has all the properties. It's not quite as smooth. It's not quite as

---

2   Absinthe can now be sold in the US, but only brands where all of the thujone (wormwood) has been removed.
3   Artemesia Absinthum, also known as Great Wormwood

tasty as the distilled product, but it will do the job quite nicely. What you do is you mix it 50/50 with water.

If you're really lucky and if you've used fresh ingredients, you will find that if you drizzle iced water through a sugar cube instead of just mixing it, you will actually get the louche effect where the liquid goes from a clear emerald green to a opaque milky greenish white. And that's really quite magical by itself.

Absinthe has a wonderful effect of giving you a very clear headed intoxication that is very good for artistic endeavors and for magical work. That's why it's my favorite. Also, if you do it to that recipe which is very close to the original Henri Pernod recipe, the stuff that Toulouse-Lautrec used to drink, it actually tastes pretty darned good too. So that's what I'm going to leave you with, how to make a legal substitution for absinthe that will make a wonderful pre-ritual tipple. Just remember, don't over indulge, because it helps to be reasonably in control of your faculties when you're trying to do a rite. So, I hope that was interesting for you.

δelⲧⲁⲓn ⲁnⴷ Sⲉⲭ Ⲙⲁⵣⲓⲥ
Episode 11, broadcast May 3, 2006

Hello, and welcome to the Crooked Path. My name is Peter Paddon and this week, we're going to take a look at Beltain, as May the first has just past us by. And of course, while we're looking at Beltain, why not have a good old look at sex and sex magic. But first of all, let's talk about the Sabbat.

Back in Europe, May Day is a very popular celebration, more so than it is here in America, probably because in America, May Day has become associated with Communist parades and Socialist demonstrations. And this week, it's become associated with immigrant demonstrations too. But in England especially and throughout Europe, May Day still has its Spring Summer transfer connotation, dancing around the May pole and having a jolly good time on the village green. And possibly the first time that the Cricket stumps are banged into the ground, and the odd ball is thrown at the willow, and people just generally make a really nice holiday of it.

It's still a public holiday in England. I don't know how much longer it'll continue that way. But it's a fun time, regardless of what spiritual path that you follow. Of course, the May Day celebrations with the May King and the May Queen and the dancing around the May pole are ritual aspects that are designed for the participation of the whole community. So they are very agricultural in intent, basically the old fertility rites so that the animals and the plants and of course the people are fertile and produce offspring, to feed us, to clothe us, to have more people to work on the fields, to feed us, to clothe us, and so on and so on and so on.

For the traditional Witch, the cunning person there is another aspect of May Day and Beltain, which doesn't get a lot of press these days, which is probably a good thing. But I'm going to talk about it anyway, because I'm that kind of weirdo.

Probably the most well known traditional Witchy thing that is done around May Day is the celebration of Walpurgisnacht on May eve. Traditionally, this was something that took place in the region of the Germany/Italy border where there is a mountain called Mt. Bocken or Brocken, I can never remember quite how it's pronounced. But on May eve, Walpurgisnacht, it is said that the Witches ride their broom sticks and fly up to the mountain to attend a grand Sabbat and to fight with daemons.

It's interesting actually because you get all these stories that are very popular nowadays about Witches consorting with the Devil at Sabbats. But the one actual genuine story that can be traced back to way back when is actually about Witches fighting daemons and devils. So there you go. It just shows what a little bit of propaganda can do for you. But it's still celebrated in Germany and Bavaria and Austria the northern parts of Italy where they celebrate Walpurgisnacht and almost have a little bit of a mini-Halloween there, commemorating the battle of the Witches against the Devil.

There's actually some really cool mystery elements that you can actually take into your modern day Witchy practice from this, because the whole thing about Walpurgisnacht is about overcoming the obstacles that you set up for yourself. It's, if you like, wrestling with your inner devil, your inner daemons, the things that stop you from getting where you want to be. And so it quite often involves taking a good hard look at yourself and seeing just exactly where your failings are.

It can be quite a traumatic experience if you do it properly, but it can also be very cathartic, very beneficial. The idea of facing up to what it is your personal stumbling blocks and finding a way to get through them. Sometimes this can take the form of breaking taboos, which is why the orgiastic aspect of it has been depicted in various versions of the legend. But more often it's got to with you just working though processes within yourself though drumming, movement, and visualization. And it is a very profound experience. Some people find it very traumatic, but ultimately very rewarding.

Of course, the real fun comes on May Day itself. In the popular celebrations of May Day, you have the May King and the May Queen selected and they basically bless the land and they kick off the party. The dancing around the May pole happens as the symbolic wedding of the King and Queen, and then everyone goes off to get completely drunk and disappear into the woods and fornicate, if they're lucky, or just go and find something else to drink, if they're not so lucky. And although this is a very literal interpretation of the sacred marriage, it does have a bearing.

The Hieros Gamos, which is the old classical term for the sacred marriage, just means sacred marriage, is all about the union of opposites. And for the practicing Witch, this often involves doing something which is very very difficult. You see, the general view of the spiritual make up of humanity is that in addition to our sort of mundane self in the middle realm, we have a darker aspect, some call it a daemon or a dragon or an animal self or a fetch beast, and we also have a higher self or a Holy Guardian Angel or a crown.

My tradition refers to this higher aspect as the crown, and the sacred marriage is actually within the self, is where the dark lower animalistic self unites with the higher more intellectual crown self. And they do that within the physical self in this realm. So you have the marriage actually of all three, the marriage of opposites within the middle ground of us as human beings, which can be a very profound thing.

And this is also very important. It is one of the key stages in the development of the Witch, because you really have to have both of these things in balance within yourself in order to craft effectively. Usually as you train as a Witch, you start off by developing. You sort of make a nod to the intellect and to the crown, and then if you're sensible, you focus on the animal side, the drake self. Then you build up that intuitive feeling, experiential aspect of yourself, but there comes a point where that reaches a limit where by itself it's not going to take you any further. At that point, you have to very skillfully and carefully negotiate this balance point between intellect and drake self, because they really are mutually exclusive under normal circumstances, because the logical functions of the intellect tend to negate the experiential intuitive aspects of the animal self and vice versa. It becomes very difficult to think when you're in animal mode and it becomes very difficult to feel when you're in intellect mode.

So the union of drake and crown, of dark and light, of Avagddu Darkwing, if you like, and Taliesin, the Shining Brow, is a very delicate operation. But when you get it right, you absolutely know that you got it right, and it actually really empowers your crafting ability and your everyday life as well. It also tends to turn things upside down, but that's another story. Well anyway, that's a look under the covers if you like of Beltain, and there's a lot more to it than just the "fertility, frolicking in the woods" thing that folklore would have us believe.

So let's turn our attention to what you really want to talk about, which is sex, or rather sex magic. Now one of the things that I want to stress, because it's been stressed the other way quite a lot lately in popular books by certain publication houses, is that western sex magic is not the same as tantra. They are connected, linked if you like, but their practices are actually quite different. They come from different cultures. They use the same energies, but they attack the situation from quite a different direction, if you understand what I mean.

Western sex magic is much more physical, I guess. Well no,

60

that's not the right way to describe it. Tantra, the way it's been popularized in the west at least, is all about delaying orgasm or multiple orgasm, and about all these strange exercises, and really western sex magic is a little bit more pragmatic. Really, every single ritual, every piece of magic that is done in Witchcraft is sex magic, because it uses the magic of polarity, the idea that opposites attract, that opposites create friction and the friction builds energy.

And this is done in many different ways in Witchcraft, cunning practice, not least by the operation of a male and a female working together. The polarity, the sensuality of the ritual does tend to build energy all by itself and that can be used very effectively. There is a lot of sexual symbolism. The chalice and the wand, the skull and cauldron, and various other things which you'll find being used, are very sensual in nature and often used in a very sensual way.

When you're working with the energy, you tend to get into a vibe where things become very sensual, and that can raise an awful lot of energy. That is the basic starting point, because magical energy is essentially sexual energy, and it has to get generated somehow. When you have a polarity, where you have the two poles, it creates a current, and that current enables the energy to flow, and it becomes more accessible. The friction is a bit like rubbing a balloon on your hair, developing static electricity that way. It's the same sort of principle but on a higher plane, if you like.

Then of course, you can step things up a notch and actually have sexual magic, which is using various types of sex acts as a form of crafting, by raising energy, or there are other ways you can do it as well.

Now one of the key things you have to remember is that although we're talking about it being a sexual thing in the physical sense, there is nothing erotic about it. Sex magic just isn't sexy. And desire is not a part of it. Aleister Crowley once said that the ideal

61

partner for a sex magic activity would be a "raddled whore" or a "bloated hag", basically somebody you are not sexually attracted to.

Some people have taken this to mean you can't do successful sex magic with somebody that you are physically attracted to. This is not true. You can, you just have to separate the two activities. You have to be able to divorce yourself from the physical attraction and focus on the work at hand, which takes a bit of discipline. This is the biggest drawback of sex magic of any kind, that it takes discipline. You have to manage to remain focused on the work at hand, and especially if the work that you're doing involves orgasm, that focus can waver at points. So you have to really really discipline yourself and be well trained to achieve that.

Orgasm releases an intense amount of energy, and if it focused and directed appropriately at the right moment, this can be used very effectively. Now in the regular sex act, if you manage to time it so that both partners orgasm simultaneously, you both have an immense amount of energy that you can direct into the crafting that you're doing.

But it is often easier actually, until you get really good at it, to not try and synchronize your orgasms, so that the one who isn't orgasming can maintain the focus and help the one who is orgasming to stay in the right place. You can actually do sexual magic where one partner is not being stimulated at all and the other partner is receiving all the good stuff, and the partner who's doing rather than receiving maintains the focus that way as well. Of course, you can do solo sex magic - it's nowhere near as fun. But then if you're in it for the fun, then you're just using magic as an excuse, and you should just get on and have good sex and forget about focusing on anything else.

Orgasmic energy can be used to charge talismans, amulets, and magical tools. It's frequently used to kick things up a notch for trance work and journey work, and you can also use it for charging up and enlivening the magical centers within the practitioner as well. So you can actually get a little bit of personal spiritual evolution going on there through the use of orgasm. See? It's a wonderful tool. You should use it as often as you can.

Of course, the most traditional form of sex magic that you'll find in old style Cunning Craft is the use of body fluids. Now we're actually going beyond what you might automatically think of, obviously semen, and female ejaculate are very very potent especially when mixed together to be used for charging things or as a sacrament.

Also menstrual blood is a very very potent tool when used correctly. There are certain things that you should use menstrual blood for rather than venous blood, and there are some things that you should use venous blood for and not menstrual blood. Not that I'm going to go into detail now because I'll probably want to do a whole subject of that by itself later on in another podcast. But suffice it to say that blood work using menstrual blood under certain circumstances can be very potent, and obviously lunar oriented work can use menstrual blood very effectively.

There are other bodily fluids as well, urine, spit, the list is endless. We don't often hear of spit being used, but it can be used very effectively. It has a certain barrier, a "taboo" quality to it that people need to work to get through, but once they get through it...

Spitting is used a lot in African magical practices, and there's no reason why you can't use it in western forms of magical work as well. Some take to it quite happily, and some don't. Sweat can be used as well, although that tends to be used as in taking the sweat of a victim - or the recipient of a healing - and using the sweat to mark the things that you are using to do the work, rather than actually trying to use it in any energetic way directly. But you have to bear in mind that the fluids that are obtained from the body, either sexually or through normal bodily functions, can be very

63

potent. Although, I would stress that if you want to practice in this way remember to practice safe hex. Don't mix or imbibe blood of other people unless you know that they are absolutely free from anything that you wouldn't want to be catching.

You want to basically treat everybody in a working group as if they are HIV positive and then you can't go far wrong. So work with your own fluids rather than somebody else's unless you're in a committed relationship with them or you both know you're clean because you've been tested and shown each other the papers. And for the duration of the time you're doing that work that you're staying away from anybody who might infect you with anything else. It's all about staying alive of course, which is one of the most magical things you can do. Please, stay alive because then you can keep listening to me.

pathworkings
Episode 13, broadcast May 15, 2006

Hello, and welcome to the Crooked Path. My name is Peter Paddon and this week we're going to take a look at pathworkings - an introduction into what exactly a pathworking is and looking at different ways of making them more effective both for the person on the receiving end and the person creating pathworkings for others. So I hope you enjoy it.

So let's get right in there and start off with having a look at what exactly a pathworking is. Basically, it's a tool which enables us to use our visualization skill to visit a place or experience an event that is not possible to do in real life. This includes visiting real places in different times, mythical places, and the realms of magic and the gods.

There are several types of pathworking, and each is used for specific purposes. In fact, the term "pathworking" is one of those specifics, although it's often used as a generic term. So let's have a look at them.

Let's start off with guided meditations. This is what is usually meant when the term pathworking is used. It's exactly what it says it is, a meditation where imagery is described and the student is allowed to experience a realm or event in a very controlled manner. These meditations are often very detailed, leaving very little to be filled in by the student, and thisis is the most traditional form of pathworking, originated as a Qabalistic technique for gaining understanding about the path of the spheres of the Tree of Life. So that's where the term pathworking comes from, from the paths on the Tree of Life.

Ok, pathworking itself, to be accurate, is literally a "path" working. The student is guided on a mental journey along a path that contains meaningful symbolism that will lead them on to a particular outcome. Details are less evident than in a guided meditation, with only the key points being given. This enables the facilitator to gauge the progress of the student from the things described during the debriefing session afterwards, things that were not said as part of the pathworking itself.

There's also the vision quest, which takes things a step further. In a vision quest, the student is led to the start of the path and is then left to journey alone. These exercises are often used as initiatory tests for students and for more experienced practitioners. They can also be used to obtain answers or lore from ancestors or from the gods, and there are several other terms that you might come across that are used for pathworkings. "Skrying in the spirit vision" is the good old phrase that the Golden Dawn used, and Journeying and trance work are used by some other Traditions.

So, let's have a look at ways we can get the most out of doing a pathworking. Well, let's start off with relaxation, because it's very important to be as relaxed as possible before starting a pathworking. The more relaxed you are, the easier it will be to actually go, and the best way to relax for beginners is to take each part of the body in turn, tighten the muscles and then relax them.

You can try it in this order. Start with your left leg, tighten the muscles and then relax them. Then the right leg, tighten the muscles there, relax them, let them go completely. Then your abdomen and stomach, tighten the muscles up and then release them, let them go completely. Now your chest and breathing muscles, tighten them up and then relax them. Your back, shoulder, and neck muscles, tighten them up as tight as they'll go and as you release them feel the tension of the day just draining away. It's a wonderful feeling. Now your head and face muscles, tighten them up as tight as they'll go. Don't worry if you're in a group. You have your eyes closed at this point so nobody can see anybody else's face scrunged up. Tighten them up as tight as they'll go and then relax them. Last, do the muscles of your arms. Tighten them up as tight as they'll go and then relax them, from the shoulders down to the finger tips.

The important thing to remember is that by tightening the muscles before relaxing them, you get them more relaxed than if you just let them go. And also don't be self conscious. As I said before, if you're in a group everyone else will have their eyes closed, so they won't see what you're doing. In time, you'll learn to relax and the more traditional beginning of a pathworking of taking three deep breaths will give you enough time to get into that relaxed state. But you do have to program yourself by doing the muscle thing while you take the deep breaths until you get the hang of it.

Make the experience easy on yourself. There are several things you can do to improve your experience. And there are some things to avoid, as well. Do wear loose comfortable clothing. Restrictive clothing can be a distraction and can also cut off the blood flow if you aren't careful. Do eat something light before the working if you are hungry. A rumbling stomach will distract you, but be careful not to eat too much. Don't have a big meal. Too much food, especially protein, will ground you out and make it very difficult to experience the pathworking fully. Too many carbohydrates and you're going to go to sleep, so you want to avoid too much of that as well. So something light, if you need to eat, but preferably wait till afterwards. Do find a comfortable position that won't cut off your blood flow. Pathworkings can run anywhere from ten minutes to over an hour. So situate yourself in a way that will be comfortable for an extended period. But if you're tired, don't let yourself get too comfortable. Ideally, don't go into a pathworking tired. You'll fall asleep. If you have to do it tired, try doing it standing up or sitting on a dining chair that requires you to sit up more. It helps to keep you awake.

Don't try to second guess the pathworking. Even if you've done it before, there can still be new stuff that you didn't see last time around. Make sure you eat something afterwards to ground you, especially if you're going to be driving.

And lastly, don't do more than one pathworking a week, unless you're being supervised by somebody very experienced. There's a very specific reason for this, because there's only one real danger to pathworking, but it's a big one that you've got to watch out for. And that is, pathworkings are addictive.

Most of us live very mundane boring lives. When we discover pathworking, it's like starring in our own movie. And students often find a great deal of satisfaction from pathworking. They look forward to them. And maybe start to do them away from their regular study. Once a week becomes two or three times a week, and suddenly they're doing pathworkings every day and beginning to loose the ability to distinguish reality from the realms. This is known as being under a glamour and can lead to health problems due to neglect, and accidents caused by walking or driving whilst not seeing the mundane world. So you really want to watch out for that. Don't get hooked, or not too much anyway.

So what can you expect from a pathworking? New students are often disappointed by pathworking until they get the hang of them, because they set their expectations way too high. Pathworking can be experienced at different levels by different people. But if it's well crafted, they will all benefit from the experience. For convenience, here's a few levels of interaction with a pathworking and the type of benefits you can derive for it.

Firstly, the day dream. The student visualizes in their minds eye what is described by the facilitator, but does not feel that they're doing anything beyond day dreaming. At this level, the benefits are mainly psychological, for pathworkings are usually created using symbolism that speaks to the subconscious mind, and lays down the foundations for future work. So it's all good stuff, even at this point.

Then you have the waking dream. Here the student is a little more involved, although still consciously listening to the narration. The student begins to notice things that are not in the narration, and maybe begins to see some things before they are described, though it is still imagery projected on the mind's eye. The symbolism is beginning to have more conscious effect on the student, who will likely continue the work in that night's dreams. This is where it starts to get really interesting.

At the next level, which I like to call living image, here the imagery begins to take on a reality of its own. While the student is still more or less aware of the narration by the facilitator, it seems distant. And the imagery is accompanied by sense, touch and eventually sound. Now the spiritual impact of the work really begins to felt, and the insights gained here will also affect all of the student's spiritual work.

Lastly, there is projection. By this stage, the student is living the pathworking as a full on out-of-body experience, and the symbolism is being worked at every level of their being. So that's really the ideal situation. A lot of people expect they are going to get the final stage right from the beginning, but you have to work up to it with experience. But even at the softest level, the level of day dreaming, it's still a valid tool for learning and exploring the magical universe.

In this section, we'll be talking about how to effectively facilitate a pathworking, how to read it and present it for people to journey with. The first thing you have take into account for this is your reading skills.

Mostly, pathworkings are written down and then read out to the students. This is really a shame, because the best ones are the ones that you can tell from your heart. They may start out as memorized prose, but they often take on a life of their own. But when you are talking from the heart, there's room for fluidity, for flexibility.

Sometimes the facilitator sees something new and incorporates it into the pathworking, which is a lot harder to do with a written script that's sitting in front of you. But for most of us, pathworkings are not done frequently enough to get away from the paper and ink of a script. Therefore, the manner in which we read them becomes very important. So here are a few guidelines for effective reading of pathworkings. Start off by reading slower. Most people have a tendency to speed up when reading aloud. This kills a lot of the potential for atmosphere. But don't read too slowly, either. Also, read lower.

You'll find that reading aloud at a slightly lower pitch than your normal speaking voice will lend resonance and authority to your pathworkings. It makes you sound more sure of yourself and promotes trust in your students. Incidentally, your voice will also carry better and be heard easier. Try varying the pace and the pitch. You're not reading a shopping list. You're telling a story. Don't be afraid to speed up and slow down at appropriate times, and let emotion into voice by varying the pitch. Few students will start snoring if you build atmosphere with your voice.

Enunciate. Make sure your words are clear. If they don't understand you, they can't follow you. Don't worry if you have an accent as long as your words can be understood. I have an accent and it actually works to my advantage. But that doesn't mean a fake British accent will give you a good pathworking technique. Well, a convincing fake British accent might.

Project. Basically, all the guidelines that apply when public speaking or performing in a play also apply here. Allow your voice to project from the diaphragm. The lower pitch will make this easier, and your voice will be heard by everyone without straining your vocal cords. As we learned in the last section, relaxation is the key to good pathworking experiences. If your students are new to the technique, talk them through a relaxation process first. If they are experienced, give them enough time to do one for themselves and remind them to do so if necessary.

There are several other things you can do, during, before, and after a pathworking to help the experience go better. Of course, some of these will not work for some students. Practice will help you decide which are the best ones to use.

Make sure the room you're in is not too hot or too cold. A little cooler than you might consider normal will keep your students alert. But too cold a room will distract them, and too warm a room will start the snoring. Try to pick somewhere without too much extraneous noise. A seasoned pathworker can journey next to a jack hammer. But most students respond better to a peaceful environment.

A recorded heart beat or gentle drum beat can often enhance the pathworking. But for a few students it has the reverse effect. So get the drummer or recording to play at the opposite end of the room from you, and get the students who are anti-drum beat to sit close to you. Often an otherwise too noisy room can be transformed by using a drum beat or even a recording of suitable instrumental music., and you can turn it into a good location that way by masking the extra sounds from outside.

Lighting should be low enough that you don't have to worry about glare in anybody's eyes. You should of course be able to read your script. Candles make an ideal source for pathworkings. Not only do they give you a glare free reading light, they add appropriately spiritual atmosphere.

A circle isn't essential for pathworkings, but certain ones can benefit from a circle being cast, and so can certain students. Use your intuition here.

Always remember to debrief fully. Get everybody to say what they got, even if they got nothing. Remember that the experience is like a dream, and the memory of it will go away if it isn't fixed in your mind by expressing it out loud.

Visualize the journey as you read it. This does take a bit of practice. But if you go on the journey as well as reading it, you'll find that you naturally pace it very effectively. And besides, it's more fun that way.

There are some basic rules to creating a good pathworking. Like any magical work, the first thing you should do when creating a new pathworking is to take a good look at its purpose. Not only will this help you to decide what kind of pathworking to create, but it will give you a basis that you can use to gather things that will enhance the end product.

But before we go into that, here are the basic guide lines to take into account:

- Always write your pathworkings in the present tense. This may seem like a no brainer, but it is very important. You should avoid past tense where ever possible, because you want your students to be in the now where the pathworking is happening. Even a phrase like, "You walk past the ruined temple where the satyrs once frolicked." will give a student the opportunity to wander off to where the satyrs went leaving your pathworking altogether. Much better to simply say, "You walk past the ruined temple." Or if you must mention satyrs, "You walk past the ruined temple of the satyrs."
- As much as is humanly possible write in positive statements. Now this has nothing to do with being politically correct.

We've all been in a pathworking where something like this has happened. "You pause by a table bearing a chalice of wine. Don't drink the wine." Almost everyone will have drunk the wine by the time you get that out. So word it in a way that warns them to wait. Like, "You pause by a table bearing a chalice, but despite being full of wine, can never be drunk from."

- With the exception of vision quests, all pathworkings should bring the student back to where they started, so the beginners can easily find their way back to mundane reality. This may sound trite, but the first time you get a natural flyer who can't find their way back alone, you'll understand just how important it really is.

- Do proof read your pathworking when it's done. Better yet, get someone else to proof it for you to make sure that what you've written can be read in a way that makes sense. You'll probably be at least half on the journey yourself while you're writing it. So typing or hand writing can get a little strange. Make sure it is actually structured into sentences before you unleash it on innocent victims.

And the last basic rule? Well, there is always a time when the rules have to be broken. Know the rules and understand them. Only then will you know when it is time to ignore them. If you don't make a habit of writing pathworkings, also make a habit of reading other people's work too. Your contemporaries in the group you work with is a good place to start, but also the "big names" - read Aleister Crowley's pathworkings and the exercises for skrying the spirit vision from the Golden Dawn.

Get books by Delores Ashcroft-Nowicki such as The Shining Path, Highways of the Mind, and The Ritual Magic Workbook. All of these have excellent pathworkings. The Shining Path is specifically paths of the Tree of Life, but the other two have a range from different traditions.

J. H. Brennan has also written some excellent books, especially Astral Doorways. Those who like the Egyptian or Celtic mysteries will find themselves very well served by getting hold of Alan Richardson's books, The Inner Guide to Egypt, and Inner Celtia.

Believe it or not, there are a lot of things you can do to enhance pathworkings that are not generally taught. Who knows why? Maybe some groups like to keep their training secret, and sometimes people just don't know that these things exist and so they don't pass them on.

Luckily for you, I've spelled out some of them below, so experiment with them. They're guide lines that need to customized to suit your own personal style, not hard and fast rules. So here we go.

At the very beginning of the pathworking, get the students to visualize a symbol that is relevant to the subject of the pathworking. Get them to see as clearly, solidly, and three dimensionally as they can. And then, when everyone has it as clear as they can, make it vanish. Leave them looking into the empty space for a few seconds. This creates a momentum to the experience, a sense of movement and expectation. They will feel themselves pulled into now empty space, and you've got them over them hardest threshold of stepping into the experience.

Early in the pathworking, you should take your students between a pair of something, two trees, a pair of pillars, even the two sides of a canyon. Pick something relevant and find some way to note it especially. There is an inherent duality to the experience of pathworking. By acknowledging this you can use it to your advantage. Just as the pillars in a Masonic temple have meaning, so does the passage between them. It is acknowledging a threshold between the mundane world and the realms that we are exploring. But it also applies a sort of psychic pressure that is similar to squeezing a tube of toothpaste. We're forcing all the potential focus and movement of the student's consciousness to go in one direction

74

by applying this two fold lateral pressure. And just like the paste in the squeezed tube, their consciousness will shoot forward into a deeper experience within the framework of the pathworking you've created. This is not to say that you can put toothpaste into a pathworking of course - well, you can, but I don't know whether it would be a lot of use. Of course, everyone would have cleaner teeth that way.

It is useful to incorporate key points at stages throughout the pathworking that serve as landmarks. They should serve some symbolic purpose. And should also if possible reinforce the whole focus and thrust of the pathworking, causing the student to go deeper with each landmark. Traditionally, these points were marked by the ring of a bell. In modern use, that might be a little distracting. But who knows? You might want to give it a try.

Limit the interaction of your students with entities, to one or two in the pathworking. This makes recall easier afterwards. And it also serves to make the point of the pathworking easier to grasp. By all means, have a cast of thousands if you need them. But keep dialog with the student to one or two key characters.

Include descriptive wording that sets the atmosphere. Don't try to tell the students how to feel, but rather set them up to feel what you want them to feel, the way a good murder mystery movie does by creating atmosphere. Describe the lighting, the temperature, the movement of objects or people in a way that conveys the desired mood. They'll figure out how they should be feeling by themselves then, which will not jar them out of the pathworking in the way that a statement like, "You feel wary." Well, that can really be distracting, when they can't see why they'd be wary.

And that is basically it. It's a very simple process that we're talking about, creating a pathworking. But when it's done correctly and skillfully, it can be a very very useful tool. So, that's the end of the final part of this particular little podcast. I hope you've enjoyed it.

pagan books and authors
Episode 15, broadcast on May 28, 2006

Hello, and welcome to the Crooked Path. My name is Peter Paddon, and this week, we're going to be taking a look at Pagan books and Pagan authors.

Now, it probably hasn't escaped your attention, but there are a lot of really bad books out there. Whether you want to talk about a certain publisher who puts out an awful lot of very bad mish mashed stuff - although, even they have some good ones if you know where to look - or whether we're just talking about the general quality of books that are being published these days on Witchcraft and Wicca, where everybody who's anybody is putting out a book with all the basics, just as if nobody had written one like that before.

So you get a lot of very basic books, and actually a lot of very uninformed drivel, being published, and very little of value to someone who's actually trying to look a bit deeper than "what is all this stuff about in the first place". So that can get very frustrating, although believe me, I would actually rather have a lot of bad books out there than no books at all.

When I first started out in the Craft way back when, there were very few books available and you really had to hunt to find them. Luckily I did find them, but they were not easy to come by in those days and they weren't cheap either. But that's just me being old, I guess.

There are a surprising number of books that are actually quite good. However, they are very basic. There's an amazing combination, really, of books that are just basically passing on the idiocy of predecessors, along with books that actually know what they're talking about, but they're talking about things from such an absolute beginner's perspective, that if you've figured out the difference between Wicca and Witchcraft, really you're beyond that sort of book.

And so, it becomes a bit of a challenge. Many of us are not lucky enough to find ourselves living near to a group. I guess I must be an exception to that because I run a group. But that's not really something I'd recommend to anybody with any sanity left either. But even when you are part of a group, you tend to voraciously hunt down books. There's something about the Pagan psyche that we are voracious readers. That's one of the reasons why many of us all love Harry Potter so much, even though he's as much trouble as he is pleasure these days, what with the fundies and the people who insist on calling non-Pagans muggles. Blurring the lines doesn't help anybody as far as I'm concerned.

But let's actually take a look at the market and see what we do have in the way of books out there. First of all, there are a lot of very good books on Wicca, which doesn't help an awful lot if you're looking for non-Wiccan Witchcraft, but you'd actually be surprised if you look carefully, some of the books on Wicca actually have useful stuff. If you go back to the origins of Wicca with Gardnerian and Alexandrian craft in England, you'll find there are some writers like Janet and Stewart Farrar who've actually done a lot of research, a lot of very interesting stuff, and a lot of the early Wiccan material wasn't that different from what we think of as non-Wiccan Witchcraft anymore.

Wicca, especially in America, has evolved into quite a different creature to what it started as with Gerald Gardener, and you'll find if you've circled with some of the "old guard" Gardnerians, some of the people that actually trained under Gerald Gardener and his immediate students, you would find that their work is much darker, much more related to what we do than it is to what your average American Wiccan does these days.

Unfortunately, just like many Japanese martial arts, Wicca came to this country in a somewhat diluted form, being handed out by people who weren't really qualified to be doing that. Now this is going to piss off a lot of Gardnerians if any are listening to this, but I'm sorry, it just happens to be the case that there are a lot of people whose linage doesn't go back as far as they think it does. Let's just say that.

There are some real books on Witchcraft out there as well. They take a bit of hunting out, because you have to be able to recognize one to start off with in order to actually know that it's worth having. It's probably easier to figure out which ones are the really bad books, and there are some fairly standard errors that you can find in a book that will tell you that this is a load of hogwash.

My favorite one is to be found in books on Celtic Witchcraft by a certain author who, amongst other things, talks about the ancient potato ritual that the Celts would practice. This of course would be a little bit of a problem because, whilst potatoes are a very big part of Irish life in modern times, they didn't actually make it across the ocean from America until the reign of Queen Elisabeth the first, and so ancient Celtic potato rituals would be something of an anachronism.

Also, you'll find that there are a lot of things that are supposition or down right fantasy that are passed on as fact. And one of the biggest mysteries, myths, what's the word I'm looking for? One of the biggest lies, let's call it what it really is, that you will find in books is the claim of Wicca, if it's a Wicca book, being an ancient religion, or of the author being part of a tradition that has and unbroken lineage back to pre-Christian days.

To be perfectly frank, who knows? There may be a tradition or two that does have a legitimate claim to an unbroken existence going back as far as pre-Christian times. But, even they will never ever be able to prove it. So, it's something that you take on faith or you take as a more spiritual metaphorical meaning. You won't find the good authors making any really big claims about their own lineage, because when all is said and done, either the ancestors speak to you or they don't, and that's the most important thing.

You will find that there a lot of people who write about this stuff and will quite gladly plagiarize the people who are good at what they are talking about. There is a certain organization that promotes Welsh Witchcraft. I won't say their name for obvious reasons. But it's a fairly safe bet to say that their claims would not stand up to close examination, and they have frequently been caught by very many people at the grand old act of plagiarism. Luckily, they haven't really had any books published. They did have some books that were privately published a while ago, but they seem to have become unavailable, which is good for all involved.

The bad books are going to generally be fairly easy to spot, because they're not going to have a lot of substance. They're going to be very big on airy-fairy rituals or telling you what you can and can't do and very little of the whys and wherefores. If you're not being told why you're doing something, you really shouldn't be doing it, because there are two things about a real Witch that you need to know if you haven't already figured it out.

The first of those is that Witches tend to be anarchists. They tend to do their own thing. So just being told to do something "because", isn't good enough. You need to know why. Secondly, and this is actually a very practical thing, you need to know why because otherwise you might be putting yourself in a very untenable situation, even dangerous situation. So, taking stuff on faith doesn't really work. This is an experiential path, and that doesn't mean that someone can say, "Oh, go try this and see what you get."

At some point, unless you have already developed a level of trust with the person saying this, and you trust that they will give you the whys and wherefores later, you really want to have those up front, because you want to know what you're letting yourself in for, and at the very least prepare for it. Sometimes you want to go where they're sending you, but it's nice to be able to prepare some cushions to land on, so to speak.

There are some books out on the market that you'll hear terrible things about, and they really don't deserve that. This is going to probably get me into a lot of trouble with people I know, but I would like to give Silver Ravenwolf as an example. First of all, her books are published by a company that is not renowned for quality work, shall we say. and she herself has been accused of basically selling out and being extremely fluffy, and doing things that are bad taste and ethically dodgy in her writings.

To be perfectly honest, whilst I don't agree with everything she writes about, her books are some of the better ones that are freely available. You can walk into a Barnes and Nobles, or any book store really, and find Silver Ravenwolf books. I've known of a lot of people who walk the path, they have walked the Crooked Path, who started out by buying a Silver Ravenwolf book. They're not high art. They're not great scholarly works. And they are about Wicca. But whether you like or loath the woman, she has made certain aspects of the craft very accessible for people when they're starting out, and it's a good stepping stone on to deeper things.

When you actually get to talk to her, in person rather than reading her books, you find that to a large extent she actually seems to have her head screwed on right with her own personal practices. I've not circled with her, so I can't say that for sure. But certainly, she talks the talk rather convincingly. So I would at the very least, withhold judgment on her, because she is providing a service even if you and I don't necessarily need that service anymore. There are those who do. And at the very least, if she is as fluffy and as money grabbing as a lot of people would like to think, she is doing us a service by keeping some of the dimwits away from our doors, while they all go banging on hers.

You know there's a purpose for everybody really, and there are other books like that. In fact one of the books that I'm going to be recommending later suffers from the bad press that the author has had prior to writing it, and this is really unfair, because it's a really good book. Those of you who've been listening regularly will have already have heard my interview with the author and will know who I'm talking about. But I'll speak more of that later.

So what books would I recommend for the average Witch in training? Well, the first one I would recommend getting your hands on is a book called *Light from the Shadows* by Gwyn. It's published by Capall Bann who happen to be the people who published my first two books, but don't let that put you off. It's a very very good book. She talks about it like she's talking about Wicca, but what she's talking about actually isn't. I used to know the author, although I will respect her privacy and not say who she is.

But Gwyn comes from a tradition that has made a conscious decision to blend old craft with Gardnerian Wicca. So she does sometimes come across as being a bit more Wiccan than you might want. But, everything she writes is very sound, and I know personally that she comes from a very good tradition. So I heartily recommend and endorse Light from the Shadows by Gwyn. It's a very easy book to read. It's very accessible, and it will really give you a good start on a path that's a little bit darker than the average Wiccan fare that you'll get in the book stores usually.

Another very good author who's sometimes maligned as being a bit on the Wiccan side because of the way she writes is Rhiannon Ryall, who is unfortunately no longer with us. But she wrote several very good books, not least, *West Country Wicca*. Despite the fact that she refers to the practice as Wicca in her books, she actually tends to be writing on a much more trad craft level than Wicca itself. She writes from a period where Wicca was the only form of Witchcraft that anybody had heard about, and so, if you

82

wanted to write about Witchcraft, you wrote about Wicca if you wanted to get it published. It was as simple as that. So you have to bear that in mind. It's probably one of the biggest reasons why good authors get maligned by the general public, is because they wrote during a time where the only way to get published was to write about Wicca, even if that wasn't really what you were writing about. People seize upon the fact that they used the word Wicca as proof that they're not really genuine, that they're fakes, and really they're throwing the baby away with the bath water when they do that. But there you go. More books for us to buy. Rhiannon Ryall - excellent author. Also, Nigel Pennick.

All of these authors so far have had books published by Capall Bann although they may have published before and since with other publishers. Nigel Pennick seems to be something of a sort of rock star in the traditional Witchcraft author circles, because he's written plenty of books. And they're all really good. Some of them are a little bit regurgitating lately, but a lot of his books are very valuable. And I heartily recommend anything he writes. Likewise, Nigel Jackson, another Capall Bann writer. I didn't actually consciously do this when I wrote these notes down, but they all do seem to have that in common.

Unfortunately, Capall Bann is starting to move away from the kind of authors that they used to have. And they're getting much more New Agey. Obviously, it's a business decision for them. But from our perspective, it's a bit of a shame, because we're probably not going to see any new authors the likes of Nigel Jackson and Nigel Pennick any time soon from Capall Bann. But then, there are those who are taking other routes to get their books published now. So don't despair too much.

The writings of the late Andrew Chumbley are well regarded. The books are very expensive and very hard going. We used to joke about him writing with an old English dictionary next to him so he could find the most obscure word for anything, because that was his writing style. However, he is a very good collector of old lore, and his book on the toad bone is very very good. It's not that you can't find the information in other places, but it's the only place where you can find everything all together in one volume. Of course, the book is somewhat expensive. It sells for hundreds of dollars on eBay when there is one available. So it's really a little bit unfair to mention him as a favorite author because unless you have an awful lot of money in the bank, you're pretty much S.O.L. for picking up any of his books these days. Since his death, they've gone up exponentially in value. I actually sold a copy of one of his books for $666, which I found very amusing at the time. But there you go.

Another author that I would heartily recommend to anybody although he isn't technically a traditional Witch, is Jan Fries. Jan Fries is actually an OTO initiate, but he's written some very very good books (of value to Witches). *Helrunar*, which is a book of runic magic, which is one of the best ones on the subject of the Elder Futhark that you can find anywhere, and he also wrote a book called *Seidways*, which is about the ancient practice of seething, or seid work, which is a type of ecstatic trance work - actually quite common by various names within various forms of traditional Witchcraft. His book is one of the best on the subject. In addition, he wrote a book called *Visual Magick*, which is part ceremonial and part traditional, very very good. He's something of a cross between Aleister Crowley and Austin Osman Spare, and his books are much much to be recommended.

And then of course, there's my good friend Robin Artisson who I interviewed a couple of weeks ago on this podcast. His book, *Witching Way of the Hollow Hill* (soon to be re-released by Pendraig) , is a very excellent book on traditional Witchcraft, and he has a couple of more books coming along which will be worth looking at as well, The Coven Book of the Hollow Hill, which is more of a practical grimoire, is being awaited with bated breath[1].

1   Published by Pendraig as *The Flaming Circle*

Then there's some books stories stories and poetry that also contain lore, that we're all looking forward to seeing when they are available. So, I'll be mentioning them when they come out. Just keep listening to this podcast and I'll keep you updated on that.

You can also find some very good fiction books which will give you some information that you can't really get anywhere. It's something of a tradition in the occult world to regard the fiction books of Dion Fortune as actually having more valid occult lore in them than her nonfiction books. *The Sea Priestess*, *The Goat Foot God*, they're all wonderful wonderful books, a little bit outdated now as far as writing style. But then, they're set in the period they were written during, so they're sort of period pieces now, I guess. If you can overcome some of the inherent sexism and racism that was a natural part of things back in those days, between the wars, you'll actually find there's a lot of great value in those books.

Also, one of my favorites, *Lammas Night* by Katherine Kurtz is a wonderful story of the Sacred King cycle and the work of Witches during World War II to prevent Adolph Hitler and his storm troopers from taking over the good old United Kingdom.

Another book which is a favorite of mine is *Way of Wyrd*, which is a very good book on Anglo Saxon magic. It was written by Brian Bates, who has since become an authority on shamanic work in the western world, and I believe he's still teaches at UCLA. Hopefully one day I'll actually make it to one of his lectures[2]. But he actually originally wrote The Way of Wyrd as his doctoral thesis. Having problems getting it published, he reworked it as a novel and had it published that way, which makes it a very very wonderful novel, because everything about it is actually real researched information that's been woven into a story, and it is absolutely magnificent. It's one of the best ways of learning about the web of wyrd and

2   He actually agreed to be interviewed on the Crooked Path, but we never managed to find a workable time to do it.

the practices of the Anglo Saxon shamans way back when. He actually followed it up with a nonfiction book called **Wisdom of the Wyrd**[3], which is basically all the background research that he did for the original book. And that is very good, too. It used to be very difficult to get a hold of. Now I believe it's in reprint. So that makes it a lot easier.

So, a fairly short podcast this week, short of reading passages to you and ranting more than I should on the bad stuff. Obviously I don't want to get sued, so I'm not going to name names, or anything like that, but I think we all know who we're talking about when we talk about the bad books. Hopefully, it's given you some food for thought and a reason to pull out your wallet, buy some more books, and show what a good Pagan you are - because all good Pagans are voracious readers as far as I'm concerned.

There are very few Pagans who aren't into reading about Paganism, though that's not to say that you can't be a Pagan if you don't read the stuff. It will raise a few eyebrows, but you can learn to live with it. After all, we're all anarchists and crazy folk anyway. So, that's it for this week, and hopefully, it has given you some ideas.

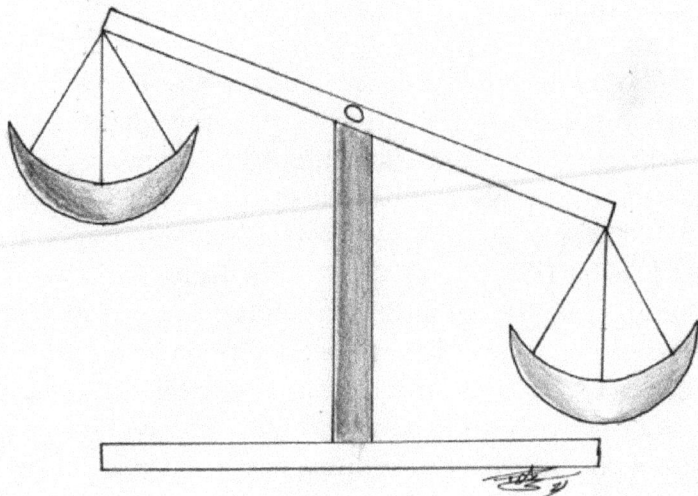

---

3   Re-released as *The Real Middle Earth*

ḱarma or Faᴄe

Episode 17, broadcast June 11, 2006

Hello, and welcome to the crooked path. I'm Peter Paddon and this week, I'll be talking about karma and fate. This was suggested by Star Belfire who wins an "oh so cool" black Crooked Path t-shirt for her efforts.

So I guess the thing we really need to do is to start off by talking about just exactly what karma is. For the average neo-pagan, Wiccan, or western adherent to some vague sort of Hindu faith, karma is more about what goes around comes around. To quote one of my favorite characters from the Victorian novel Water Babies, "Do as you would be done by and be done by as you did." from the teacher lady who's actually two characters. But then when have I ever been able to count?

This is probably best described as a very very simple way of looking at cause and effect, and it extends into the realm of reincarnation. Karma and reincarnation in the mind of the average neo-pagan are very closely aligned, because karma is said to extend beyond this lifetime and into the next. You can be working through karmic debt from a precious lifetime in this one, so it's very confusing.

With it being so tied up with reincarnation, I guess we had better take a quick look at reincarnation too. Now the popular concept of reincarnation made very popular by all the Llewellyn books and by various other modern day publications, documentations, web sites, and television programs is the idea that everybody when they die, they get a little vacation in Summerland, and then they get to choose a body to be reincarnated in. They come back to the mundane realm as another person. And somewhere in the process of getting into that other person, they have their memory of their former lives erased, and so they can start again from scratch.

But they have a set of lessons that they've chosen to learn in this particular lifetime, and it has some interesting ramifications. For example, if you follow this doctrine of reincarnation, then suicide is a big big no-no, because the doctrine doesn't really treat suicides very nicely. The basic concept is that if you commit suicide to get out of some issue in this life, then in the next life you'll be put back to deal with exactly the same issue, but you'll have it a little bit harder. So, it's probably a good idea to stick around and try and get it right the first time. Heh, heh. That's just me being evil.

The biggest problem with this concept of reincarnation is that it's been heavily polluted by western modes of thought, that says that everybody has the right to be whatever they want to be, and all men are created equal, and so on and so forth. Now technically speaking, all men *are* created equal, but, it doesn't stay that way for very long, because we all have different abilities and different problems, and that makes us all pretty unique and we're not all the same. That's something we should be all very grateful for.

Likewise, we don't all automatically get the right to reincarnate. When you actually look at the real concept of reincarnation, as practiced by the Hindus, it's a lot more complicated than that, because the idea of reincarnation in the Hindu faith is much more to do with recycling than being born again as it were. The concept is that when we die, the essence of who we are and what we are gets basically put into this huge melting pot, and becomes part of a cosmic soup from which ladles of new humanity are poured forth. And so, whilst we do get to come back, we don't get to come back as a single entity.

The idea is that we just get recycled, which is an interesting concept, but it actually makes a lot more sense if you think about it. Now this actually ties in very well with what the"Celts" believed. There is a lot of evidence to show that the Brythonic Celts of Wales especially had this concept of the Cauldron of Ceridwen where we all go back into the cauldron when we die, and it's only the most elite and special people - who have earned the right to reincarnate as whole entities - who are able to climb out unscathed from the cauldron. Everyone else gets boiled down into the soup and recycled.

This is really an important thing for me. It's a very key part of the Tradition that I follow, the concept of the Mighty Dead. These are people who, through acts of heroism, great spirituality, military leadership, or great artistic ability or creativity, earn the right to join the ranks of the Mighty Dead. They end up becoming the great teachers, the great bards, the great characters of history and mythology. And you and I really have got a long way to go before we get there. So, it's soup for us, I'm afraid. And that's not necessarily a bad thing. The basic idea about the soup is that all these components get pulled out in different combinations, and it's, if you like, the powers that be are looking for stable combinations. And when a combination is stable, it creates the scenario where that person is able to qualify to become one of the Mighty Dead, and then they continue on.

The whole idea of this is that we often think of spiritual evolution as being something very much on an individual basis, but as far as the universe is concerned, one individual's spiritual evolution isn't that important. The most important thing is spiritual evolution of the race as a whole, the species as a whole, and so this concept of trying out the combinations and recycling gives us the best of all worlds really, because things that don't work, that aren't promoting spiritual evolution, are going to get cleaned out.

So Adolf Hitler got put back in the soup, so, we don't have to deal with his spiritual debt, as it were, from his actions polluting the over-all spirituality of the human species. However, the bits that went up to make Adolf Hitler get recombined with other pieces and maybe they come out better in the long run. And meanwhile, you have these people who are doing these great heroic or spiritual acts or great creative artists becoming eligible to reincarnate.

It's not a conscious decision on the part of some overwhelming judgmental God or anything like that. It's just a matter of when the combination of parts is stable, and you get thrown into the cauldron, the parts don't fall apart and you don't join the soup. You stay whole and complete and are able to climb out of the caldron again. It's as simple as that. It's pure and simple metaphysics. I guess that's the best way of describing it.

Now, this then enables these people who've managed to retain their integrity and come back as themselves for several lives, to be the great teachers. And their spiritual level is elevated because of their status. And they are also, through being role models and actively through teaching others, able to raise the spiritual level of other individuals. And this gradually brings the whole of humanity up to a higher level of existence. That's the theory anyway. Despite the evidence that you see around you, with violence, wars, and G. W. Bush, I firmly believe that is true. The human race as a whole is becoming more spiritual, more self aware, more awakened. And this is very important, because that's what it's all about.

The really cool thing about the Cauldron and the Mighty Dead of course, is that it ties in with the mythology of Gwyn ap Nudd and the wild hunt. In most Welsh traditions, it is Gwyn ap Nudd and his wild hunt who come charging around at Samhain to collect up the souls of those who've passed away during the past year, to escort them into the mound, to Summerland, and ultimately to the Cauldron and the soup. So there you go. Now you know what's for supper.

The whole idea of karma and the "law of three", "threefold return" and all that, is not really where I'm coming from, if you haven't already figured that out by now. The important thing to remember is that all these laws are constructs, conventions to help us to understand something. And one of the biggest mistakes we can make is taking these things as literal laws of nature. The "law of three" was supposed to say that what goes around comes around.

You're going to push energy out into the universe and chances are sooner or later it's going to come back and bite you on the butt.

This is why traditional Witches, cunning folk tend to work more from the concept of doing what is necessary and paying the coin, taking responsibility for your actions and being prepared to pay the price. If you're not prepared to pay the price, then don't do the deed - it's as simple as that. For us, karma isn't really a concept or term that we would use. We'd be more inclined to talk about Fate.

Fate of course is a much maligned word these days, because people tend to look at the concept of a fatalist. You know, this is the way it's going to be, this is the way it's meant to be, you can't dodge your fate. It's like a bullet with your name on it and sooner or later it's going to catch up with you. This is not a popular way of looking at the universe. People like to look at the concept of free will and say, you know, I can do what I want. I can choose my life. I can choose to avoid certain traits within myself and to improve myself. And to a certain extent, you can, within the dictates of your fate.

This is something that on various online lists there have been huge arguments about. The idea that Fate is what dictates the way we live our lives and that the concept of free will is to a large extent an illusion. Those of us who use the concept of Fate in our world view, we often talk about the Queen of Fate.

The Queen of Fate is the mystical fourth face of the Goddess, if you like: Maid, Mother, Crone, and Queen. So we actually have four faces, because we look at things a little differently in case you hadn't guessed.

The Queen of Fate is an interesting concept because she is often seen as cold and merciless. Arianrod is the Queen of Fate in Welsh mythology, and she is seen as being quite cold and merciless, especially in the story of Llew Llaw Gyffes her son, where she cursed him with three geasa: that he will never receive a name unless it comes from her and she isn't going to give him a name (and Uncle Gwydion and Llew get around that one); And then she curses him that he will never receive arms, which means he can never be an adult unless she gives them to him and she'll never do that (and Uncle Gwydion and Llew manage to work around that one); then finally, she says that he will never have mortal bride -and Uncle Gwydion and uncle Math get together and build him a Flower Maiden so that he can have his jollies, sow his wild oats as it were. Ha, ha.

And a lot of people see Arianrod as being this cold hearted bitch who tries her best to make his life a misery, because he showed her up by proving she wasn't a virgin, by making his arrival in the world at the moment of her being tested for her virginity. Of course, this is another case of taking things metaphorical as literal truth, and what we're really looking at is the concept that if she had just given him these things, they would have been more or less meaningless.

So she had to do what she did, he was fated to have to work for them, to earn them if you like, make them his own. And she gave him actually a very great gift, because the ultimate result of her gift to him was his own immortality and his place the constellation of Welsh deities, which of course, from my perspective are the ones who are the best. But you might disagree with that if you're not into Welsh deities.

The whole concept of free will, is it reality, illusion, or both? Well you know, there is an old tale that if you ask any two Witches for their opinion you'll get three answers, and this is very much a situation where that is the case. Free will is on the face of it, an illusion, because we are guided by Fate, and we are fated to be who we are, and to do what we do.

But actually there's a lot more to it than that. Like most things in Witchcraft, the reality is a little more complex than the simplistic truth. One of the things that you have to take into account of course is that many things in Witchcraft involve the resolution of paradox, and the subject of fate and free will is no exception.

Paradox for those who didn't swallow a dictionary for breakfast is where two things are totally incompatible. An oxymoron is a phrase that is a paradox, like military intelligence, because the two just don't go together. Paradox is like traveling back in time and killing your grandfather. It creates a paradox because if you killed your grandfather, then chances are you would not have been born and therefore you could not have gone back and killed your grandfather, which means that you would have been born, which mean you could have, and so on and so forth.

There are a lot of things like that in Witchcraft, paradoxes, and the trick is that when you have to reconcile two apparently opposing and incompatible things, that third thing that creates the harmony between them is the thing that is generally true. This is illustrated by the flaming lantern or flaming torch between the horns of Baphomet. And so we talk about the flaming brow of Taliesin being an example of that too. So, free will is for most people an illusion. You think you have free will, but really you're just following your predestined path.

Of course, the role of the Witch is traditionally to cheat Fate. Once again, there's a paradox there, because how to you cheat fate? You cheat it by surrendering to it, by working with it. It's almost like some of these martial arts moves, like in Aikido, where you use the strength of your enemy against him by bending and going with the flow. And this is exactly how it works, by surrendering to Fate and accepting it, you can transcend it and therefore cheat it, except it would be your Fate to transcend it, so it's not really cheating, if you see what I mean. It gets very complicated talking about it.

The best way to describe it is the way I did on an online discussion on a Yahoo list with Robin Artisson, who you may remember from my interview a few weeks ago. We were discussing Fate on the list, and there were lots of arguments to-ing and fro-ing. I finally put in my five cents worth, and it seemed to go down pretty well, so I'll share it here as well. The basic idea is that at any given instant in time - time of course being relative and a paradox all by itself - at any particular instant you are fated to react the way you react. Whatever happens right now you are going to be reacting to it totally predictably because you will react the way that you react to it. There's nothing can change that.

However, you can, with an awareness of this, gradually transform who you are in such a way that you would react differently. And so, whilst in the instant, you are bound to react as your Fate dictates, and there's no way around that, you have to bear in mind that Fate is not something that written ahead of time. There is no past, present, future. It's all a cosmic now. And so, Fate is constantly being written as you do it. So, all it's really saying is, rather than saying from the moment you were born you were destined to be hit by a bus at the age of fifteen, what it's saying is that if you don't do anything to alter who you are, then that will happen.

But, maybe on the way you become more spiritual, and you become more aware, and therefore whatever the event was that led to you stepping in front of that bus in the initial scenario, is changed. It's not a very good example, but it's about the best I can do really without waving my hands around. You being able to see me wave my hand, somehow that makes it make much more sense. But, the basic concept is, to reiterate, that whilst Fate is written in stone, it is written in stone instant by instant, and so it is only in that instant that you are bound by it.

How it gets written is down to your level of awareness, your level of spirituality, your level of effort if you like. So you can actually work with Fate, surrender yourself to Fate and work within its parameters and overcome the limitations of what would have been your Fate had you not been awake and aware and a Witch, which I think is very important. So if that made any sense at all, I'd appreciate somebody letting me know, because I'm always trying to find a way to make it succinct and easy to understand.

So that's it for this week, and I'm going to be recording next week's one very shortly, because next week I'm going to be in London and I'm not really going to have a chance to do it in my normal manner at the last minute. So I'm actually preparing ahead which is a scary thought. See? I have overcome my Fate of being a lazy git. So until next time you hear these dulcet tones, have a good week and I'll talk to you again soon.

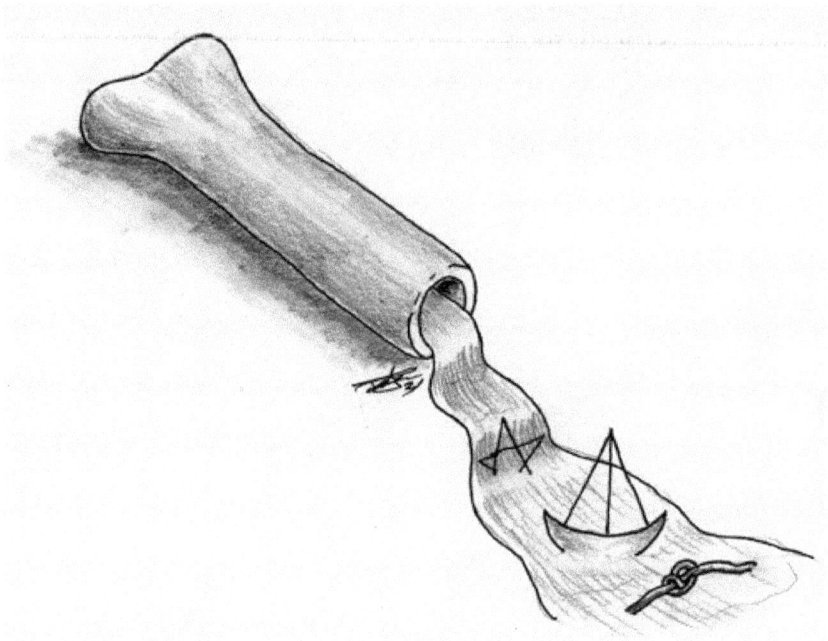

Tapping The Bone

Episode 19, broadcast on June 26, 2006

This is the Crooked Path. And I am your host, Peter Paddon. Jen Snow suggested this week's topic, tapping the bone or recovering Lore through ancestral workings. For that, she wins a suitably wicked black Crooked Path t-shirt.

So we start off with the age old question, "what on earth is tapping the bone?" Well, tapping the bone is all about ancestral memories, basically the concept of tapping into the knowledge and wisdom of those who came before us, because all that information is stored within us. Whether you think of it as memories tucked away inside your DNA - there's a lot of people that support that theory - or whether it's something more ethereal that is connected to your genetics and to your blood line, but in a more subtle way.

Either way, it works really well for me. There's a lot of terms that are used for this form of ancestral memory; the Bone Ladder and River of Blood are two favorites. They're used a lot in the tradition I follow. We talk about being immersed in the River of Blood when we are actively recovering the Lore and information that can be gathered from the ancestral memories.

The Bone Ladder, of course, is a nice image. We're not talking about boning, for any of you little perverts who are thinking otherwise. This isn't a sex magic class. This is a discussion on ancestral workings. The Bone Ladder - a lot of the symbolism that is associated with ancestral work has to do with bones, skulls and such like - and even the phrase, "tapping the bone" of course, conjures up the white shiny stuff in its imagery. There's actually possibly some theoretical truth to the concept of the memories being stored in the bone rather than any other part of the body, because bone, although it is a fibrous sinewy hard calcified sort of substance, does consist of a matrix of crystalline molecules. It contains a lot of crystalline structure within it. Those of you who have listened to me ranting on about the use of stones and crystals in magic will know that crystalline structures at the molecular level can take on the properties of energy and thoughts by being basically whacked whilst surrounded by that energy - it's called a sonic shock, and it's a form of imprinting.

I think that maybe there's something connected with this that is why there are so many phrases using bone or skeletal symbols to represent the ancestral memories. It's also of course metaphorical as well, because the skeleton, the bone, is the structure upon which everything hangs. And very much for those of us who follow one of the old non-Wiccan Witchcraft traditions, everything we do tends to hang upon the Lore of the ancestors. It's one of the more interesting parts of the way things go together.

We tend to have a unifying structure to all of our Lore and practice, which means that everything flows a little bit better. I think that's one of the reasons why traditional Witches tend to go for the rituals coming from the heart rather than having things heavily scripted, because everything we do facilitates working that way.

The River of blood, of course, is a gorier sort of image, but the whole idea of bloodline is being immersed in your bloodline, being totally and completely connected with it. And at that point, the Current is around you, within you, and there is no way you cannot be open to the Lore that passes by and through you. And so, this is a very important concept, that can actually lead to some interesting practices if you think about it carefully.

Now, one of biggest things that people tend to forget about ancestral Lore and ancestral memories is that, well to put it bluntly, they're nonlinear. You're not going to get a time progression that makes any sense. You're not going to get past, to present, to future. Most people wouldn't be expecting the future, but as I said in previous podcasts, the whole concept of working with ancestors is totally tied into the nonlinear thing of time. Time is nonlinear. We just experience it in a linear fashion usually.

What this means is that we can have ancestors long gone and ancestors yet to come, and we can tap into Lore and memories in all directions. So that potentially complicates the issue terribly, but at the same time it also raises some interesting possibilities. Personally, I really don't care whether the lore that I recover comes from past, present, or future as long as it is valid, and the validation is done in the trying it out stage.

Remembering forgotten Lore is a very important part of what we do. It's almost impossible to believe that anybody could have a tradition that has an unbroken lineage from pre-Christian times these days. Every tradition, no matter how valid or genuine, has had a hiatus somewhere in its history. At the very least, the need to go underground to avoid persecution by the Christian church has often led family traditions, the real ones, to assimilate and conceal themselves in what appears to be good Christian Lore. And that's one of the difficulties, of course, that in modern times people automatically see any Biblical references in practice and they say that's not really Pagan, is it? And truth be told, it probably is more Pagan than anything from anyone who claims unbroken lineage, because the real old trads are going to have that. They're going to have a mixture of Christian Lore thrown in that has been used to either augment or replace even the more Pagan Lore from previous times in an effort to maintain the survival of the family and of the line.

There would also be a lot of, I don't want to use the word "infiltration", I'm trying to think of a better one, but there'll be a lot of "input" from other types of traditions. For example, a family trad that has indeed survived from renaissance times is probably going to have a hefty dose of Renaissance magic of the John Dee variety thrown in for good measure, because that was what was fashionable at the time. Anything that survived from back then is likely to carry some of that with it, and a lot of people would see that as a contaminant. I actually see it as verification that maybe they actually have some validity to their claims.

Of course, any real tradition wouldn't waste their time trying to convince people they have an unbroken lineage, or even a broken but venerable lineage, because they have more important things to do. So every tradition, young, old, venerable, or based on a book -and there's nothing wrong with that as long as you're honest about it - we're all in the game of trying to recover lost Lore. We all have a body of Lore that we work and study and practice.

But, there's always going to be gaps that we're looking to fill, probably for ever and ever, because every time you fill gaps it opens up a new gate and through that gate is, guess what, more gaps. So that's one of the reasons why this is a lifetime study. Wicca, you can get to be an HP and HP-ess in three years, and you pretty much see yourself as an elder and a teaching person and ready to pass on your wisdom to the young 'uns as they come by.

I was reading an article today about someone who's been in Wicca for seven whole years and was talking like a venerable elder. Let me see, I've been doing this for particular tradition for six years now. I've been initiated six years in this tradition, and I had training before that. I had eleven years as HP of a Wiccan coven, and three or four years of training before that, not to mention my personal study between the age of twelve and eighteen. All that and I'm far from being an elder.

I think that is another one of the keystones of a traditional Witchcraft group, is that the good ones look at eldership as something that is bestowed or you earn it after many many many years, and not just because you got a third degree initiation.

There's a lot of techniques for remembering forgotten Lore, and we'll talk about some of them. But the important thing to remember is that you don't take anything as gospel, just because it came in a trance session doesn't mean it's right. You always try to validate and verify anything.

The ancestors being what they are and wanting this Lore to be recovered, they tend to help facilitate that. So they will point you in the right direction to start off with. You can always validate Lore by trying it out, talking about it, discussing it with people who are experienced in your tradition, and then taking it to the floor and working it and see if it works.

See if it works, and also whether it fits in with the nature of your tradition. I mean, something can work perfectly well, but maybe it isn't in tune or in harmony with everything else you do. So then you have to decide. Do you change what you do to harmonize with this new thing, because it's really amazing and cool? Or do you say, well yes, this is a valid thing. Maybe we'll pass it on to someone who can use it, but it's not really our cup of tea. Well, that's probably one of the harder things to do. When you've got a really cool piece of Lore that works, but it isn't really working as something that can be an integral part of what you already practice, it's really hard to say no, I won't use this. But you have to be realistic, and you do have to try and be objective as much as you can be in a subjective subject like magic. That of course is all part of the fun.

So on to practical bone tapping. How do we go about tapping the bone and picking up that lost Lore the ancestors have left lying around for us? Well, there's a couple of different things you can do. I'm going to go over three simple exercises and try and give you an insight, so that hopefully you can work out some of your own as well.

One of the things that is very important for doing ancestral work is an ancestral altar. Now, the important thing here is that you actually create your ancestral altar not as a shrine, but as a working tool, and probably the best way to describe it is to give you an indication of some of the things that we use. I mean, our main working altar is an ancestral altar.

We always work with a hearth stone because it is a meeting point of the family, past, present, and future. The hearth stone is where everybody comes together, to bathe in the warmth of the hearth or the heart of the family. And so, we always have a hearth stone on our altar. Sitting upon the hearth stone is a skull. Now this can be a real bona fide human skull. If you do choose to go that route, please make sure that you get one legally, that is buy one from a medical supply place. They're fairly expensive, but they have the benefit of coming with documentation, so when you get raided, you don't get charged with the murder of some unspecified person.

The other option, a safer option, which is still just as effective, is to use a representation of a skull. We actually use a resin cast skull that has Celtic knotwork all over it. It's very nice and looks like it's made of pewter. And it really doesn't matter. You can use bone clone, which is a plastic, very realistic looking skull. Just make sure if you do get raided, show them the imprinted, embedded, bone clone logo in the base where the vertebrate meet the skull. Heh, heh, heh.

We have a lot of other stuff on our altar as well, but I won't bother going into that because really the important thing is the skull and the stone, and frequently a candle. We tend to use two candles that are specifically for ancestor working. There's a red candle, the fire candle, and the blue candle which is the candle of the winds, and that usually sits on top of the skull. That probably knocks out the possibility of using a plastic skull, because you don't want to melt it. But, the trick here is to actually work with these as a tool, and we work with them every time we craft, because we always activate the ancestral altar, which we do fairly simply.

We always pay coin for the space when we do a working. That coin gets placed on or beside the hearth stone, until the end of the working where it gets given up at the crossroads. So that's how we start off. We start off with bringing the coin and we tap it on the hearthstone three times and place it on, beside, or under the hearthstone depending on where it seems to be the appropriate place to put it.

Then we light up the fire candle with something like, "Fire flame in the old ones name, light and dark turning, luck be in thy burning.", or words to that effect. And we also call our Horned Master at that point, our Horned Lord, not to be confused with the satanic majesty of the Christians, although many people do confuse him with them.

Next, we light the blue flame upon the skull top with, "To part the veil and let us in to the realm of the ancestors." At this point, we then call upon the ancestors, usually grab a wand or stick of some sort, bang three times on the table, and invite all ancestors to come and be present. Then we focus upon the skull, and we breathe life into it. We use pranic breathing. There are lots of different names for it... in eastern traditions there is a form of breathing called pranic breathing which imbues the breath with life force. That, technically is a similar sort of thing to what were doing, but being western and pragmatic Witchy Cunning Folk, we don't really want to rely on the eastern terminology.

Basically, what you do is you crouch down so that the skull is at eye level and you start to focus upon it and focus upon the ancestors. As you breathe in and breathe out, you feel the life force filling you, the ancestral force filling you right down to the bottom of your boots. When you finally can't contain anymore you "aaaaaaah", let it out, breathe the breath of life into the skull, and feel the ancestors take possession of it. And believe me, you can actually physically feel it when you get it right.

At that point, the altar is activated and is ready to work, and it will help guide you in your crafting. We also call upon a specific ancestor for our tradition. For obvious reasons, I'm not going to share that part with you. But you'll find that as you do ancestral workings, there is one particular ancestor who will become a representative to your group, as it were, almost an ancestral guardian. It's a good idea to call them by name to bring in the other ancestors, because that just adds to the strength of the whole process.

When it comes to summoning ancestors, apart from when you're activating the altar, you can actually call in the ancestors. Now Robin has written some very good articles on this, Robin Artisson in his book and on his web site. A very simplified sort of précis of all that would be that you basically fill yourself up with fire, the fire of the ancestors if you like.

You can stand in the center of your sacred space, and as you breathe in and out, you see it as almost as if there's, the enclosure in which you find yourself is a giant sort of bellows. It's not so much you breathing in and out, it's the bellows that are pushing the air in and sucking the air out of you. You basically use that bellows breath to fan the flames of the embers of your hearth until it bursts into bright fire, and then you let that leap up and take hold of your body and blood and spread through your body like wild fire. You literally have your blood metaphorically boiling within the veins.

And when you feel totally inflamed, with every exhaled breath you start to just push it down into the ground, essentially getting deeper and deeper each time, until finally you make contact with the molten fiery center of the earth. Then you draw up some of that fire back into yourself and let it revitalize you, and when you feel totally inflamed and totally there in the moment, you call upon the ancestors to attend you and to share with you their wisdom and their knowledge and their lore. And that's the simple way of doing it.

You can actually do a lot of other interesting things with it as well. But I can guarantee you, you start doing that on a regular basis and you'll find you get results. One of the things we really like to do is after every fire festival, Sabbat, cross-quarter, or quarter working - or whatever you want to call them - we like to have a session, a couple of nights later, where we call in the ancestors, and we do an ancestral oracle.

What we basically do there is we set up the ritual space, and we get ourselves all fired up, in a very similar manner to the way I've described. Then you sort of stretch your neck out, move your head forward, tilt your head down. Basically, what you're doing is you are opening up the area of the base of the skull, at the back of your neck. You set your guardian, your patron deity if you have one or the guardian of the circle, whatever deity that you work with in that capacity, to stand guard at the gateway of your skull. Then you invite the ancestors in, vetted of course by your guardian, your doorman as it were.

Before you get to that point, you sort of exhale in your visualization a purple haze, an amethyst mist that fills the space around you, and then you call the ancestors and you have them all standing behind you. Then your patron or guardian sort of acts as doorkeeper and lets appropriate ones in, and you just let it go. If you do this in a group, it's good to have someone who doesn't actively participate so they can take notes or report or whatever, and you just basically let the ancestors speak through you.

That's why we call it an ancestral oracle. It works really really well if you let it. The hardest thing, like in many forms of trance work, the hardest thing is to get out of your own way. Don't try and analyze what's going on, you can do that afterwards when you debrief.

So that's a couple of interesting practical exercises. I'm sure if you think about it, you can take those and run with them and come up with some new and interesting ones of your own.

Interview with Dave Finnin

Episode 22, broadcast July 17, 2009

Hello and welcome to The Crooked Path. My name is Peter Paddon and this week we have with us Dave Finnin, the Magister of The Clan of Tubal Cain in America and well known curmudgeon, and a very interesting guy who's probably the closest thing to being able to give us a "from the horse's mouth" account of Roy Bowers, also known as Robert Cochrane, and The Clan of Tubal Cain/1734 stuff. At least as close as you can get without getting a Ouija board out and having a séance. He has the advantage of being corporeal, so we can pick him up on the microphone, which is why he was our first choice. It would have been nice to have interviewed Roy Bowers himself, but obviously there are certain technical difficulties involved in that.

Peter Paddon: So, thank you for agreeing to submit to this ordeal Dave.

Dave Finnin: Alright, alright. They took the trowkin out of the room now, so I'm ok. I can talk freely.

Peter: We do have a small audience of invited strange people, who are gazing with rapt admiration at the fact that we've managed to get it cool enough not to melt in here. So let's sort of just kick straight off and talk a little bit about Robert Cochrane. A lot of people got very interested in Robert Cochrane and The Clan of Tubal Cain from various articles and arguments going on on the internet, but for a lot of people he seems to have sprung up out of nowhere, suddenly appearing with a few magazine articles that inspired Joe Wilson to write to him and then the whole letters thing happened. Could you tell us a little bit about some of the background, some of the origins?

Dave: Ok, well, Robert Cochrane was born in 1931. His real name was Roy Leonard Bowers. He was born on January 26, 1931 to a Methodist family in the London area, but about his early life I don't know too much. I do know that he and his wife at one time worked on the canal systems with the river people and that's where he first got involved in some of the folklore of magic and so forth, from them.

Later on for a spell he was a blacksmith, which brought that whole influence for the Tubal Cain. In the early '60s, I don't know the precise date, but I've been able to confirm it with several Gardenarian contacts and others, he was initiated Gardenarian. He worked with a Gardenarian coven in London. He had a boat on the Thames River in London and one of the Gardenarians I know knew him there, and made an athame for him, and we've seen an artifact, a candelabra he made for the main coven.

Peter: Wow. You get the impression from some of the people writing about The Clan of Tubal Cain that it existed in perpetuity from sort of Pictish men running around with spirals tattooed on their bodies. How long was exactly The Clan of Tubal Cain active in the UK?

Dave: As I understand it - this is from Evan John Jones - he met Roy in 1964. His wife was working in the same firm as Roy and that's how they met and, according to Evan John Jones, Roy had had another group working with them two years prior, the previous two years, so the actual time was about four years active operation of The Clan of Tubal Cain.

Peter: Oh, cool. Is it still active now?

Dave: This is what was interesting, when we went over to England in 1982 and were put in touch with Bill Gray, who then put us in touch with Evan John Jones, we didn't think there was any interest at all in Roy. Fortunately Bill Gray, it turned out, not only had an extensive correspondence that nobody had seen with Roy, but he also had worked with him.

Consequently we went to see Evan John Jones, who was living in Brighton, and I guess we interested Evan John Jones into reviving a little bit because he undertook to teach us - we did it by phone and by letters, for two years, went back to England again and were formally brought into the Clan. At that time, Evan John Jones had no interest in running a clan so he made Ann and I Magister and Maiden, and he basically, no, he didn't basically, he actually wrote down that he was under us in The Clan because at the time he didn't want the responsibility.

Peter: So it wasn't just the US, it was the Clan period.

Dave: At that time yes. In the 1990s, when Evan John Jones was interested in doing more of the Shamanistic, the Sacred Mask, Sacred Dance, the animalistic things, which was a path we really weren't interested in pursuing; we wanted to get more in the primitive God forms not the animal. John got some people around him and in the late 90s he started up the Clan again in England, as we understand it.

Peter: There are different versions of the story about Doreen Valiente and the infamous plate with the numbers on it. Can you tell us the story as you know it?

Dave: I've heard the story from three, maybe four different sources and all of them pretty much agree on the basic points. Doreen found the plate, which said 1724 on it, it had a rough sketch of a rooster on it and some other things, in a pawn shop or thrift store there. She gave it to Roy. Roy decided it would be a good little gimmick to use to put over his story with Justin Glass in her book. So that's basically it. The story is true, the plate had nothing, absolutely nothing, but Roy decided to elaborate and go on from there.

Peter: I know a lot of people take it as gospel that the number was actually 1734 and that's where it came from. It's really one of those wonderful areas of argument that you find online.

Dave: I should explain that when Roy was writing to Joe Wilson, he was talking about 1734 and it was not a number it didn't mean a date, it wasn't an address or anything, it was based primarily on a Goddess name, an attribute, which he was influenced by that by a book called *The White Goddess* by Robert Graves. As a matter of fact, I'll tell you even a little more. You go to Robert Graves, you look up the sacred alphabets, and you pretty much got all you need to work it out.

Peter: Cool. Likewise there are also many opinions surrounding the death of Robert Cochrane. Whether it was an accident, a planned ritual act, or murder or suicide. I think just about every possible variation has been touted as being the truth at some point. There is supposedly a suicide note that was found. What is your understanding about the circumstances of Roy Bowers's death?

Dave: Ok. This is from both Bill Gray and Evan John Jones, each have a slightly different variation of it, but basically because Roy got involved with another lady who was allowed into The Clan of Tubal Cain, his wife Jane left him. This was in May, on May 11, 1966. Both Bill and Evan John Jones believed that he wrote letters to his friends and even to his lawyers, telling them he was going to commit suicide. I think he did that with the hope that they'd rescue him and bring his wife back to him.

We do know that Doreen said that Roy had met with a couple of clan members in a pub on Saturday, June 18th and Evan John Jones knows that Roy came over to his place on Sunday the 19th and they sat around and talked for a while, and Roy made some comments about how his life was in the lap of the Goddess, and he may be working on the other side, but at the time they didn't know what he meant. He left about seven that evening and Evan John Jones, when I saw him, still had the tie he left behind that day.

So that's the last they saw of him, however on the 23rd of June, which was, I believe, a Thursday, Roy decided to take a mixture of poisons. Belladonna, Librium tablets, and a root called Hellebore and he took these, ingested them. The next day, Friday, the police were notified by a solicitor, his lawyer, and they went to his house, looked in the window, and saw Roy in a sleeping bag on a couch and they broke in. He was comatose. They found a note from him, addressed to the coroner, explaining what the mixture was he took, and even in the note it said something to the effect of "Being of a sound mind, but you may not judge that, I have done this to myself. He went to the hospital. Roy died nine days later, at 5:30 on Sunday July 3rd.

Peter: I know it's an area of, has to be, of pure speculation, but do you think he was planning not to succeed?

Dave: That's the feeling that, I mean if you read Doreen she said that he'd sent her a letter, he'd sent his wife letters, he'd sent his solicitor letters, I think he was hoping he'd be pulled back. But, you know, I don't know.

Peter: I guess until we have that séance we never will know. In addition to the letters that Joe Wilson gave you copies of, you went to England yourself and trained with Evan John Jones as we've heard and were initiated into The Clan of Tubal Cain, as well as talking to and receiving additional letters from William Gray. Could you talk about the differences between The Clan practice and the practices outlined in the letters, obviously without going into any awkward areas, you know, don't give away any secrets. Are they quite similar or wildly different?

Dave: Okay, first, the letters were more a philosophy. If you read the letters there's very little, what we call technical ritual information,

111

in there on how to do things. Roy, in his letters to Joe Wilson, was using him as a sounding board with some theories of his own and so forth. He wrote five letters to Joe Wilson, and I believe it was three, some people say four, to Norman Gills.

It was over a dozen letters in the correspondence to Bill Gray and Bill Gray he was very specific about what they were doing because he treated Bill as an equal, whereas others sort of like students or people he's putting on a little bit. I've always thought the 1734 as explained in the letters was a philosophy, it wasn't actually a tradition, it wasn't actually a detailed way of doing anything, just some hints and some feelings. The Clan of Tubal Cain, as both Bill, Evan John Jones, and even Doreen wrote about and experienced, was a gut instinct, acting more on emotions and a lot less rhetoric and getting in there and doing a rite, letting the answers just come to you, go into a trance state and actually doing it. So it was not something you could really write out in detail.

Peter: Quite a big difference then.

Dave: Definitely.

Peter: With Evan John Jones no longer with us, you're probably the person that has the record, well you and Ann between you, for the longest continuing practice as Tubal Cain initiates still living. How long has it been you've been practicing now?

Dave: Since we started as Tubal Cain, both as students and later taking it over, in 1982. Prior to that we were working Roebuck, which used 1734 as part of it, but that was since 1974.

Peter: So the Tubal Cain stuff has been 24 years at least now. That's quite some going. Have you ever thought of writing a book about your tradition and your experiences?

Dave: Ann has written a manuscript[1]. She has to update it. I don't know if people are interested because it's out there, people have seen copies of our training manual we use to teach people of our basic, what we call the Roebuck, system, which has incorporated more and more of The Clan as years go by because we found The Clan was sort of the roots of what we're working with and have been working with. We can't really separate them the way we used to.

Peter: Well that makes sense. Ok, so Dave now we're going to open up the gates of hell and let these demonic beings lurking on their chairs here ask questions.

Dave: Fine, I've got my protective circle out and I got my charms on, I'm all set.

Peter: So let's see, who should we let have first swipe?

Audience: I see that you brought some cords with you Dave; can you explain what those are?

Dave: Alright. I have in front of me a short red cord with what they call a monkey paw at one end and a noose at the other. This is just worn around the neck. This originally had the Witches knot ladder in it. This was left with Bill Gray, this was Roy's cord. When we were handed over The Clan of Tubal Cain by Evan John Jones, Bill Gray gave this to us, gave it to me, as I was taking on the role of the Magister. In ritual we untied all the knots, released any of Roy's spirit connected with it. I keep the cord to remind me of the tradition and to keep it true[2].

Peter: Very cool. Ok, next?

---

1   This was published by Pendraig as ***The Forge of Tubal Cain***

2   I was present at PantheaCon 2008, when R. J. Stewart confirmed that this was, indeed, Roy Bowers' Magister cord.

Audience: What drew you to the teachings of Robert Cochrane, Roy Bowers?

Dave: It was a different philosophy. The letters were what we first saw. The original coven Ann and I were initiated in was the Mohsian tradition, Bill and Helen Mohs. At the time they called it The American Trad, but it's now known as Mohsian. Among the information they had were the letters from Joe. Joe gave them the copies of the letters and also some Regency material and this came to us along with our initiation and the Book of Shadows that the coven used. We read this and we saw something deeper than just the Gardenarian influence that was in most of the other traditions going on at that time. This was in 1974.

We had our own small coven, it was sort of an outer court where we were training students and so forth at the time, and we were starting to incorporate some of that philosophy into what we were doing. In 1976 we formally decided to name the coven, we called it The Roebuck, and if you're familiar with the Cochrane letters you know how we got the name.

Peter: Okay, who wants to go next?

Audience: How has the way you've use these teaching manifested and how do your ways of working compare with The Clan of Tubal Cain?

Dave: What was the first part of the question?

Audience: How has the way you've use these teaching manifested?

Dave: Through trial and error. Beyond that I don't know how else to answer it. It's a case of you try something, we combine things, we build up our quarter system and we had a lot of input from many different people. Joe Wilson also contributed a great deal, his former wife Mara, who'd worked with us, contributed and helped us balance out the system and a lot of people that were dedicated students and initiates of ours over the later years.

Peter: And next.

Audience: You mentioned before The Regency group, it was founded by some members of The Clan of Tubal Cain after Cochrane's death, how, if at all, are you influenced by the rites of this group?

Dave: We're not really. I've got a few the rites of The Regency, but they were basically... the Regency was a group that did public rites, it didn't do the private, deeper discovery type of rites which we were interested in for self-discovery, it was very much public rites, The Regency. So it was not something we actually emulated at all.

Audience: What do you think of the recent explosion of interest in The Clan of Tubal Cain tradition?

Dave: Well, there's a lot of interest in it. The trouble is, most of it seems to be a crossing of wires, some people think 1734 and Clan of Tubal Cain are the same thing. I might as well explain it now, if you look at Joe Wilson's website or if you've read it in the past, Joe is very, very definite on there; 1734 is his tradition, it's an American tradition. Clan of Tubal Cain was Roy Bowers, or Robert Cochran's, tradition as he practiced in England. I could go into the many differences, but if you read the 1734 letters there's not a tradition in there, there isn't a set way of working rituals in it, it's a philosophy.

Peter: Ok, so now let's take a slight change in direction and talk a bit more about 1734 and about your own coven, The Roebuck. Start off with, just to reiterate in case people weren't listening earlier, is it true that Roebuck existed prior to your trip to England and did it predate your receiving the Cochrane letters?

Dave: The Roebuck originally was called The Passing of Training coven, started in 1974, about the same time we were initiated originally by Bill and Helen Mohs in what is now known as the Mohsian tradition. A part of the information that Bill and Helen had was the letters that Joe gave them, so we received those letters, plus, very shortly after we moved from Pasadena at the time to where we live now, Tujunga, we were right across the street, couple blocks away from Joe. We worked with Joe and Joe gave us some more information too on it. This was in the 1970s. I mean we didn't get involved with The Clan of Tubal Cain until 1982.

Peter: I've just seen on various websites and forums people occasionally referring to Roebuck being founded by the letters, which is quite an interesting concept by itself, or being founded by Evan John Jones, which is also quite interesting. So, I just make sure that everyone listening is absolutely clear on this; The Roebuck is its own thing and has an existence of its own.

There does appear to be a wide variation between the different covens who work 1734, working with the papers obviously. You sort of touched on this already, but is 1734 really a tradition the way people describe it or is it more of a movement?

Dave: It's a tradition now, but up until the 1990s when Sandy and Doug Kopf started working with and formalized it as a basic foundation of ritual way of working and so forth, it was more a philosophy, at least in my opinion. The people I knew that had the letters and so forth, were all working various other traditions and various other ways of doing things and they'd incorporate a little bit of it into that.

Peter: Can you tell us a little bit about how the 1734 papers came to be spread so far and wide.

Dave: Two words, Joe Wilson. You talk about a little bird pollinating from pod to pod to pod, that was Joe.

Peter: You do seem to bump into the papers in the most unlikely places.

Dave: That plus the fact that Joe, on his website, decided to put the papers up on the website. When he put them up there, I must admit I looked at them and I saw a difference between what he put up there and what we had in the original letters, so I figured, well he did it there so I'll put it up on our own website, so I made all the papers available including the stuff we got in 1982 from Bill Gray.

Peter: And I understand there's at least one coven in England now working the 1734 papers, that I came across on a web search recently.

Dave: Well, I wouldn't doubt it. As a matter of fact, we're quite open and we just claim the work. The papers are very useful for giving you a kick in the philosophy, you know kicking you into a little higher plane of thought and consciousness, but as a tradition in themselves, they aren't.

Peter: Some say that there's a lot of material in the letters that was actually put there to pull Joe Wilson's leg and Cochrane certainly had a reputation as a trickster. Do you think that readers have to be careful about what they read into the letters or do you consider them to be a fairly reliable source that can be wholly trusted?

Dave: You treat the letters as what they were and that is a sounding board of a philosophical, spiritual theology from Roy to Joe. I mean, we never saw what Joe wrote him and basically it was one side of a discussion. You just take it for what it was there.

Peter: There's also been a certain amount of haggling over ownership, copyright, etc. of the papers, with even different version of the letters, as you've alluded to, being freely distributed for such a long time. Are they public domain because they've been available?

Dave: As I understand it, the Byrds-Bernes, the Swiss city where the formal copyright thing was agreed to, the United States signed that in 1985, the letters have been in the public domain since 1966 in the United States. Almost 20 years, I'd say it's pretty close to being public domain by 1985. So I consider it as public domain. We've yet to receive one letter from Jane Bowers, or her solicitors or anybody about it and we've had it on our website for years[3].

If you can still find the letters from Joe's site, compare them to what's on the cyberwitch site which we allude to for our own website, 'cause that's where we put the information. Just judge for yourselves, I think if you look in the letters you'll find there's more symbols in the set we had than in what Joe put up. What we couldn't understand is when Joe's second wife, Mara, left him, Joe was despondent and so forth, had been drinking a little bit and he decided all this Paganism at that point had caused his trouble, so he burned all his papers. A couple years later, we gave him the copies we had, so he had the same copies we had. So I don't know what to tell you about what he put up there, why it was different.

Peter: There definitely seems to be a great deal of interest in traditional Witchcraft in general, and I guess the 1734 papers and what's known about Cochrane is the most easily accessible material for people to catch on to. Do you get a lot of inquiries about the materials?

Dave: We do, and I usually recommend that they read Doreen Valiente and Evan John Jones book *Witchcraft: A Tradition*

---

3   Certain parties in the UK did serve "cease and desist" letters from their lawyer in mid 2009, to the Finnins, their web host and some others, but on being challenged to prove their case, they withdrew the claims.

Renewed because that gets more into how to do the type of rituals that Roy did and get into the philosophy of it than anything I've seen out there really.

Peter: Cool. So, just before we close up, let's see if anybody has any questions for Dave about 1734 and The Roebuck. Who wants to go first? .

Audience: You guys have been quite active in the Los Angeles area for some time, you have several daughter covens now; how many are there out there practicing The Roebuck?

Dave: Well, off and on, at the maximum we had five daughter covens. Somewhere Ann has got a garter belt, which we made up, with the silver symbols for five covens on it. Right now it's down to about three actually working. Covens are sort of interesting. If you look at the history of them, they average about five year life spans, a lot of them. We've only managed about seven times that ourselves.

Peter: Yeah, I think it's fair to say that even in covens that do have longevity there tends to be heights and depths to them, where they'll have a period of a lot of activity and students and all sorts of things going on then they'll have a couple of years where they're sort of recuperating from that before they gird their loins and start all over again. Does that sound about right?

Dave: We had a couple of the covens in which the High Priest and High Priestess broke up. They separated, that demises the coven. We had another one that had a serious illness and some financial difficulties, so they're somewhat inactive. We've got one up in Ojai area that is going like great guns, is attracting people, and has been going for several years now. We've got another one that's sort of half dormant. And our own of course, we've still got The Roebuck going, it never stopped.

119

Peter: Yes, they'll never stop The Roebuck. So, who's next?

Audience: How do you see the 1734 tradition and The Roebuck developing in the future?

Dave: I can't speak for the 1734 tradition as such, because you can't really point to anything, you can say you have people working based on the 1734 letters, but what that is as a tradition I don't know. As for The Roebuck we've been, since 1980 when made our connection with The Clan of Tubal Cain, we've been incorporating more of The Clan of Tubal Cain in it, more of Clan stuff has worked its way into our rituals for The Roebuck and it keeps evolving. It's a living thing. Every time we think it's more or less set in concrete, it changes.

Peter: With any old traditional form of Witchcraft, if you don't like the way the tradition is, wait, because that is one of the big differences, especially over here in the US. Traditional covens tend to grow and evolve and the Wiccan covens tend to set everything they have in stone and become very dogmatic. That's really one of the primary differences.

Dave: Well, let me interject something I learned when I was in England. Now I may have the number wrong, but Gerald had at least five High Priestesses'. Each of them had covens which operated different from each other. So you might say that sort of shows the same thing.

Peter: Yeah. Well that's why I specified America, because I know my own experience of Gardenarians in the US versus Gardenarians in the UK, you almost can't recognize that they're supposedly the same thing because there's a very different attitude, different way of working. You do have to be careful that you specify which lot you're talking about really. It's a bit like the OTO; you have to specify which OTO you're talking about. Anyway, who's...? Yes.

120

Audience: I have question about books. For those who go to the bookstore looking for something more meaningful or something for a deeper spiritual seeker, what books would you recommend that person read?

Dave: Okay. First of all, on history, the book I recommend for history is *Triumph of the Moon*, that one's good. For the American version of it's a book called *Drawing Down the Moon*. For spiritualists, I get a little bit faint cause I'm not into the more radical feminist movement, but *The Spiral Dance* does give you a lot of the spiritual movement, the spiritual behind the Goddess worship.

Peter: And next, what have we got?

Audience: Is there anything you'd like to say about the challenges to your lineage?

Dave: Well, so far I've yet to get anyone that was actually willing to face to face challenge me, because I'd show them not only the written letters from Evan John Jones, we also in '91, our last time over in England, we sat down and did an interview with Evan John Jones and I got it on videotape. So, there's no denying what we got, if you wanted just to confirm it look at the book that Evan John Jones and Doreen Valiente wrote, Witchcraft: A Tradition Renewed, which deals with the whole Clan of Tubal Cain workings, Dave and Ann and the Roebuck are dedicated in that and discusses us in that book, the things we did. We gave John an athame, we brought a candle over, which we went up to Roy's old site and we burned it up there.

Peter: Well of course nobody will go face to face with you; they know you'd have a cannon and various forms of armament. They're afraid to be outgunned.

Dave: Everybody knows I'm not confrontational at all. I'm supposedly the reclusive nobody can talk to. I don't know how. I've been using my real name all these years, not one of these pseudonyms or nom de plume or anything else. Dave Finnin is Dave Finnin. You go on the internet and do a Google search on me you'll find the good, bad and the ugly on me.

Peter: Yeah, I have to admit he was very difficult to track down, we had to walk all the way up that hill to his house. Any other questions? Well in that case, we'll lay this beast to rest. Dave I'd like to thank you very much, you've been very entertaining, very informative.

Dave: Keep that fan mail coming.

Peter: Thank you very much Dave and Ann for your time and thanks you the demons of the assorted levels of hell for joining us and asking your questions. That's it[4].

---

4   Please note that the opinions given in this interview are just that - opinions given by the interviewee. Their inclusion here does not imply an endorsement or agreement by the author, who is quite capable of having his own opinions.

Oaths and Pacts

Episode 23, broadcast on July 24, 2006

Hello, and welcome to the Crooked Path. My name is Peter Paddon and this week, I'm going to be taking a look at oaths. Now oaths is a subject that can raise blood pressure and so on and so forth. It's a word that's associated with secret societies such as The Golden Dawn, The Freemasons, the Rosicrucians, fraternities, and with all the negative implications that can have with some people.

The idea of swearing allegiance comes difficult for some people especially in this country, because everybody has such an independent spirit. And when you actually look historically at some of the oaths sworn by members of certain secret societies - the blood curdling oaths spelling out dire consequences for anyone who breaks them - they're enough to give you sleepless nights if you read too many of them, to be honest.

Probably the granddaddy of them all is the oath of Freemasonry which apparently includes the immortal phrase, "to have your tongue ripped out and your throat cut and your heart plucked from your chest", or something like that, anyway, really nasty, physical, murderous things to happen. Even in Wicca, the oath talks about, "and if I betray this, my solemn vow, may my weapons turn against me and may I experience that death of the soul which is absence of the presence of the Goddess" or something like that. It's been a long time since I've done a Wiccan initiation, so, I can't remember it too clearly.

But anyway, it's the idea of making hidebound promises with dire consequences for breaking them, that's really quite off-putting for some people. I know a lot of people in the general Pagan community have taken the attitude, "Why do I want to do this?" And you know, I can quite understand that. In Freemasonry and organizations such as The Golden Dawn and the Rosicrucians, the Builders of the Adytum, and the OTO, the oaths are there to protect the secrets of the order, not because destruction will rain down upon the earth if it gets into the wrong hands, but it's more a sort of proprietary thing. It's a copyright issue as much as anything else. This is our stuff. Keep your mitts off. Of course, they don't portray it that way.

I seem to remember in Aleister Crowley's autobiography, he talks about having to take this blood curdling oath to become an initiate of The Golden Dawn, this great oath of secrecy, and as a result of taking that oath and being initiated, he is then proudly presented with the Hebrew alphabet. It's a little bit of an anti-climax, if you see what I mean. So why do secret societies have oaths? Well, unfortunately for some groups, they tend to be more a tool of control than anything else. If you have sworn an oath, you are in danger of at the very least of being kicked out of the group if you break that oath, which means that they have leverage on you. They are able to make sure that you don't talk about what goes on, so that people don't learn that it's really just a drinking club, in the case of certain fraternal organizations.

In other circumstances, maybe there's things of dubious legality going on. After all, the Freemasons are not unknown to have had their lodges used as bases to foment rebellion, not least the rebellion that resulted in this country in which we live, the good old United States. And that's a very important thing to consider. But there's also a lot of mystique associated with oaths and secret societies, and so a lot of people actually join them purely for that reason. On other occasions, you have organizations like P2 in Italy which was a major political organization within the Freemasons, not necessarily organized as part of The Freemasons. But a couple of people who were Freemasons took advantage of the oath of secrecy to set up a society within a society to undertake dubious doings of a political nature within Italy.

That became quite a scandal when people broke their oath and had the punishment part of their oath fulfilled. I believe one of them, whose name escapes me, was found killed in the classic Masonic way, according to the oath.

Of course, your average Wiccan coven isn't going to quite do that sort of stuff to you. But they are going to hold it over you if you disagree with them. Sometimes oaths can be badly misused. Luckily, I've never personally experienced that, but I have heard stories. Probably the worst way, or the most common way rather, that oaths are misused is in the case of empty promises.

An oath is normally a two way thing. You promise to keep the secrets and follow the rules and in return they actually are supposed to give you some secrets and give you some benefits of membership. And quite often, oaths are just plain not worth taking in many organizations, because you're not going to get anything of value in return. There are a lot of covens out there who will give you the traditional blood curdling oath to take upon your initiation, and there's nothing they're going to teach you that you can't find in a book for yourself. And that's really a sad state of affairs.

It's a comment on the Pagan community at large that there's an awful lot of empty shells out there unfortunately. But that's part of the process when you, a serious student who is finding out what's the good sources. And for me, the important thing is to actually think very carefully. When you come to a point where they're asking you to take an oath, if you haven't already started asking questions of yourself, now is the time to do it. You want to ask yourself, "Do I really want to bind myself to these people? Are there any red flags that tell me I shouldn't? Do I feel comfortable putting an obligation upon myself to these people, to align myself with them? Are these people whose behavior is something that I aspire to within myself? Can I see them as role models? Is there anything just that makes me nervous about this?"

Well that last one - there should always be a yes answer to that, but in this case I mean in the sense of feeling that something isn't right. You really do need to look at this.

Any organization that takes you into an initiation, and does not let you know what the oath is going to be before you have it presented to you to actually say, that is a time to walk away. You do not want to be putting yourself in the stressful and very emotional situation of an initiation and that point come across the oath for the first time as somebody reads it to you a line at a time for you to repeat. You need to have a copy of that oath before hand to actually read through it and make sure that you are actually willing to say it. If there's anything about sexual favors, well it's up to you whether you go ahead with that or not. But obviously anything you don't like, don't dismiss it out of hand.

Talk to the High Priest or High Priestess or Magister, or whatever the head of the group is called. And express your concerns. "You know, I'm not really happy with the way this is worded. Can you put my mind at rest?" And if they fly off the handle at that point, it's a good time to say, "Ok, I'm walking away now." But they might give you a perfectly acceptable explanation of what it means, in which case once again if you have no problem, feel free to go ahead. But don't be afraid to walk away if it doesn't feel right.

Taking an oath and joining a group just because you want to be a member of a group is not the right reason. You need to know that it's the right group for you. And you need to know that it, more importantly, that it's not the wrong group for you. So, take that into consideration and think very carefully before you agree to take any oath with any group. And always walk into it with your eyes at least half open.

So what about oaths in a Traditional Witchcraft Coven? Well, that's a very good question because obviously with traditional Witchcraft, you don't tend to get a lot of details about other traditions. So most of what I'm going to talk about is relevant to my own personal practice. But I think in general it applies across the board.

One of the things that I do know is that there are oaths in traditional Witchcraft. And depending on the nature of the tradition that you're following, they can be one of several types. Most groups of a traditional nature tend to talk about a rite of adoption or of fostering or of bringing into the family rather than initiation. And so the oath often reflects that. It's more of a statement of family than anything else. Also, whilst in Wicca and the ceremonial magic orders, the oaths tend to be a matter of pledging allegiance to the group and to the leader of the group, oaths within a traditional structure tend to be more of a pact between yourself and your gods, your ancestors, and so on and so forth.

There is a lot less of the "You are my fearless leader and I will follow you no matter where." Because the nature of traditionals is that they're a fairly ornery, independent bunch and they're going to follow their own path anyway. So trying to tie someone down with an oath to following somebody else's line isn't going to be very convenient or very useful.

One of the really big differences, I think, is that while the ceremonial bunch tend to be very big on making their oaths all about secrecy. You swear to keep secret their deep dark deeds. In traditional covens, you tend to talk more about silence than secrecy. Silence is not so much never discuss these things as don't talk about them inappropriately. Silence is matter of using your intelligence and using your intuition and using your common sense to see whether it is appropriate to discuss the subject. So it's not an all out "thou shalt not talk of these things". It's more of a case of think about who you talk to. And use an appropriate level of discretion when you're doing that. So silence rather than secrecy which is, I think, a very important difference.

The first oath you're likely be asked to take in a traditional coven is an obligation to your gods, a pact with your patron or with the deities of the tradition in general. A pact with your personal deity is most common. It really doesn't have anything at all to do with the group that you're learning with, and that's exactly the way it should be. So you're not placing yourself under any real obligation to the group. You're placing yourself under an obligation, into a relationship between you and your gods, which of course is a very serious matter, if you're taking a thorough approach to your path. But it is a significant difference. You're not kowtowing to some other human being. You're very much establishing a relationship with the deity so that you can progress on your personal path, regardless of whether you stay with the group or not. And that's the whole point.

For want of a better description, the first admission, the induction into the group for fostering is a sort of trial period that you're entering. You've probably done a year or so of training as a seeker, pre-dedicant and dedicant at this point, which means you're getting to the point where you're ready to start learning. So you're taken in as a fosterling to the family so that they can start to share with you the experiences that will help you to formulate your path.

And it may be that as time goes by, you discover that your path doesn't coincide with the group. So they leave it in such a way that it is perfectly ok for you to leave the group at some point when you or they discover that it's not the place you need to be. Most ethical groups will do their best to help you find a direction, your path, as you walk away from them. They tend to be very helpful that way.

Another really big difference between Wicca and traditional Witchcraft as in Wicca, everybody gets to be a High Priest or High Priestess if they want. It's very much a "if you want it, you can do it", the very Roman idea of "everybody is equal", everybody has the same rights, and if they want it, they should be allowed to have it.

In traditional Witchcraft, this is not the case. This is the narrow path. This is the road less traveled. It's the path for the few. And that's not meant in an elitist sense, it's that most people aren't not daft enough to want to walk down it.

So, people start down this path for one reason or another, and discover that it isn't for them. We help them on their way to find what does work for them.

So you start off with an obligation to your gods. The next step on the way a bit later on is the obligation to your ancestors. You make a pact with your ancestors. And at this point I guess, it's more of a formal induction into the family. This is where the rite of adoption takes place. And it can be done very simply.

In my own group, we almost don't have any formal structure to this at all. We under go an exercise during which the ancestors either accept you or not. And if they accept you, you are in and the bond is assumed and implied at that point. There is no ambiguity to it, and we don't dress it up with fancy words, but it's just simply there. Then of course, obligation to your ancestors can often be tied into an obligation to your coven or group. Not absolutely one hundred percent necessary, but it is quite common for that to be part and parcel. After all, you're forming an allegiance, forming a bond, a pact with the ancestors of the tradition, and that by definition includes the fellow members of the coven or group.

So there is that bond of support and service there as well, which in a good group is not really stressed. But it's there and it works in a very dynamic way, and the whole thing is tied up.

I mentioned ethical groups. Probably oaths are the most obvious area where ethics have to be one hundred percent kosher. If a group is being unethical about their oaths, then you can pretty much guarantee that they're not going to be ethical about anything else either, and you want to run screaming from them as fast as you can. The oath is a pact. It's a business transaction. It's a two way thing. You have to remember that. No matter what the wording, it's always a two way thing.

You are making an obligation, and they are making an obligation back, whether it's the gods, the ancestors, or the people in the group. So it's very important that honor is honored, for want of a better phrase, that everybody is able to keep the word that they make. And this is one of the reasons why the grandiose statements and threats of punishment are really irrelevant, because if you break this oath you are breaking your pact with your deity, you are breaking your pact with your ancestors, you are shattering any chance you have of continuing along your personal spiritual path for this lifetime.

And so, really you bring about the punishment on yourself rather anybody else having to impose it on you, and that's why oaths in this kind of group tend not to include the blood curdling punishment, because they're not needed. If you screw up, break your oath, become a warlock, you're fucked anyway. You're not going to get anywhere by doing that, because you cut yourself off from the gods, you cut yourself off from the ancestors. What is left of your path to follow? Because they're so bound up with each other, you cannot follow the path without the gods, without the ancestors. By whatever way you perceive them, they are part and parcel of the path. And so cutting yourself off from where you're meant to be is actually a very terrible punishment and you do it to yourself. So, remember that.

Lammas

Episode 25, broadcast on August 7, 2009

Hello, and welcome to the Crooked Path. My name is Peter Paddon and this week we're going to take a look at Lammas, Lughnasadh, "lug nuts", "Loaf Mass", and hanging on the tree. It is the fire festival that takes place at the beginning of August, give or take, depending on which version of the Sabbat wheel you're using, or what calendar you're using even. The date can vary a little bit, but it is known as Lammas in old English, from Loaf Mass the Catholic festival, which is based on Lughnasadh which is the Irish festival of Lugh, which is a celebration of both Lugh's birthday and a wake for the death of his mother.

So basically, he was miserable and they put a contest on to cheer him up. It's also, for those of you more mystery school inclined, it's also the time of the trials of Lugh and Crom, which is an interesting Lord of Darkness vs. Lord of Light seasonal battle that takes place at this time of year.

Lugh of course, is the Irish god of light. Some people call him a solar diety. It's not really particularly accurate. He's more a god of light, of various forms, not just solar. And of course, he's also the master of all trades, which makes for an interesting life. He is the Grand Artificer, if you like. And for that reason, he's a very interesting character to work with.

For those of you who haven't figured out by now with these podcasts, my patron is Llew, which is the Welsh equivalent of Lugh. And we'll be getting to him in a little bit. Most people celebrating a Pagan wheel of the year tend to go for the agricultural aspects. And for Lugnasadh or for Lammas, the agricultural aspect is the first harvest. This is why the golden haired Lugh is seen as the first ear of corn that is sacrificed, and whilst this is a very agricultural thing, the idea is that the ears of corn from that first piece are saved to sow in the field for the next year. But there is a deeper mystery to it, because it's also a lot to do with the concept of Lugh as sacred king. And so we'll be taking a good look at that.

First harvest, first sacrifice, except for some of us it's actually the second sacrifice, but we'll explain that as we go along. To start off with to give you a little bit of understanding, I'm going to switch over to the Welsh version of Lugh which is Llew, two Ls, Llew (pronounced ch'Looh). Llew Llaw Gyffes. He's a lovely boy, and he battles with Gronw for the love of his wife Bloedwedd.

There's an awful lot of lore and mystery tied up in the story, and it happens to be the primary myth that my own group uses for the Sacred King cycle. So I'm going to tell you my version of the story. It may be a little irreverent, but I'll be the one getting kicked in the ass by the gods, so don't worry about it. Just listen and enjoy.

The story basically starts with Math son of Mathonwy who is the king of Gwynedd at the time, looking for a new foot-bearer. He has this interesting condition, sort of militant athlete's foot or something like that, where he can't put his feet on the earth except for during battle, so he has to keep them in the lap of a virgin to maintain the peace, otherwise he'd be in battle all the time I guess.

The previous owner of that position had gone off to get married. And obviously didn't want to retain her credentials for the job, so basically he was looking for a replacement. Arianrhod turned up applying for the job, she was the sister of Gwydion, the court magician.

Math said, "Well, can you guarantee that you're a virgin?" and she said, "Oh, yes. I'm a virgin." So he says, "Well, in order to prove this, you have to step over my wand." She stepped over his wand and not only did she prove that she wasn't necessarily a virgin, although there is some argument to that case, she did promptly deliver of a child, and the child upped and away into the sea, and was later named Dylan and became an interesting sea deity.

But meanwhile Gwydion noticed a little lump of nothingness that had also fallen out. Heaven knows what it was, but he scooped it up and hid it in a chest, and it eventually developed into a young lad. He tended the young lad, and when the kid was formed enough to be recognizable, he presented the young lad to his mother, to hopefully have a tearful reunion. But Arianrhod was not very happy about this, and she spurned him.

And she laid a curse upon him that he would have no name but the name that she gave him, and she would never name him. This is a pretty serious deal for a young Celtic mythological-type lad, because a name was very important in Celtic society. So anyway, off Arianrhod went and Gwydion decided that he had to help his nephew get a name. So they dreamt up a pretty interesting little plan.

Basically, he disguised himself and the young lad as cobblers, and they set up their shop on the beach below the castle of Arianrhod, Caer Arianrhod. Through his magic - Gwydion was a great magician and twixter, sorry trickster not twixter, he didn't eat candy bars, not that I'm aware of anyway - he made the seaweed look like leather, and made an old wrecked boat look like a cobbler's shop.

They started making these wonderful fancy shoes for everybody, and eventually Arianrhod found out about these wonderful shoes that were being made, and decided she wouldn't mind a pair. So she sent a handmaiden down to get her a pair of shoes.

And Gwydion said, "Well you know, I do need some measurements." So, the hand maiden went back and measured Arianrhod's feet and came back with the measurements. And Gwydion deliberately made them just that little bit too small, so when they were sent up to Arianrhod, they pinched awfully, they were a little tight. So she

133

sent them back down saying, "Thank you. These are absolutely gorgeous, but they're a teensy bit on the small side. Could you put that right?" So he made another pair.

This time he made them just a little bit too big, so he sent them up and Arianrhod tried them on and lo and behold, they were too big. She sent them back saying, "Now they're too big. Can you make a pair the right size, please, idiot." And he said, "The only way to do that is to actually measure from your feet directly. So you'll have to come down."

So she came down to see these cobblers. And they were beautiful shoes, very well made. And, you know, not unusual for size to be an issue. Heh, Heh. Puns not intended there. So she comes down to the beach, and the first thing she sees is the young lad throwing stones with remarkable accuracy at the seagulls. She says, "My, what a radiant youth with sure arm."

And Gwydion said, "Great. Thank you. That's what we came for." She says, "What do you mean?" And he says, "You just named him, Llew Llaw Gyffes, Lion mane of the strong arm." He had flowing golden locks like Prince Charming, I guess. And she said, "Ah! You tricked me, you bums." Then she said, "Well, you won't be able to get around the second one. My second curse I lay upon him, that he will only bear arms if I give them to him. And I shall never give him arms."

Now we're not talking about the funny things with fingers on the ends that come from your shoulders. We're talking about spears and swords and such like. Once again, it's very important in Celtic society, part of the rite of manhood is the receiving of your arms, once again, the weapon-type arms. So, Gwydion and the newly named Llew went off to ponder what they were going to do about this. Eventually, they came to plot a wonderful plan. They disguised themselves as bards, because one of the other interesting facets of Celtic society in general was that it was extremely bad luck

134

refuse bed and board to a bard. It's all those Bs, you see. It played havoc with the language.

So they disguised themselves as bards and went knocking on Arianrhod's castle door, when all the men folk were off fighting a battle. They were invited in and given hospitality, food for supper, and a bed for the night. And in the middle of the night, Gwydion got up and he, through his magic, made it sound like there was an attack going on on the castle. Of course, all the men were already off fighting another battle, so, all the servants were roused and everyone was sort of clamoring around, and Arianrhod too.

Gwydion says, "Well, give us some. If you've got any spare arms and armor, give them to us and we'll go out and help fight." Arianrhod said, "Yes, of course we have some." He says, "Well, you deal with the lad and I'll get your handmaiden to take care of me."

So she strapped on the armor onto the young lad and gave him a spear and a sword, and Gwydion said, "Ok, fine. We're done now.", and starts taking his off. She says, "What are you doing? There's a battle", and he says, "well, there's no battle. It's just an illusion. But you've just presented arms to your son." She yells, "Ah! Ya bugger!", or the Welsh equivalent, and basically said, "Ok. Well, this last one you're really not going to get around. He shall never have a mortal wife. There, try and wriggle out of that." And so, off they go.

Gwydion decides to pull in King Math, at this point, and they started discussing what do. In the end, they decide that if he cannot have a mortal wife, then he shall have an immortal wife, and they construct for him a maiden out of nine different types of flowers. And it's the petals and leaves and pretty scents in the garden, not the white sort of powdery stuff that you make bread out of.

They constructed a maiden who, when they breathed life into her, was given the name Bloedwedd, a beautiful name, Bloedwedd,

135

very Welsh. Llew was promptly married off to Bloedwedd, and he became lord of his own land and generally life was pretty good.

Except, being leader and having a very busy life, he was often away from home, and Bloedwedd, of course, was very young, although fully formed and mature in body, in her mind was a little naïve, because she hadn't been around very long, because she'd come into life fully formed as an adult.

She got lonely without him, because he was off hunting and doing court and stuff like that, and she ended up becoming enamored of a hunter who came by, called Gronw, and they spent way too much time together.

She began to resent it when her husband did come back, because she wanted to spend more time with Gronw. They became lovers, and so she began to plot on what they could do.

Now she knew that Llew was a deity, and so he wasn't going to be an easy person to kill. In fact, he was going to be almost impossible to kill, because there was only one way that he could possibly be killed. So, she and Gronw hatched a cunning plan.

One day, she was sort of sitting there making small talk with him, and she says, "You know I'm really really concerned." And he says, "Why is that?" She replies, "Well, I'm worried that you're going to die." Llew says, "Well, there's no way I can be killed" but she responds, "That's not true and you know it."

He tells her, "Ok, there's one way that I can be killed, but it's so unlikely, it's never going to happen", and she says, "well, I just keep dwelling on it. I can't get it out of my head, because I just know something terrible is going to happen. Maybe if you told me how it is that you can be killed, then I could put my mind at rest knowing how unlikely it is."

He answers, "Ok. Well, basically I have to be neither on the ground nor in the air, neither on land nor in water, neither under a roof nor under the open sky." And he went on on all these various things.

At the end Bloduedd says, "Oh, I see. That is pretty unlikely. So, you've put my mind to rest" and Llew says, "Great. Let me read the paper, catch up with the news, and get on with my life."

So anyway, a couple of weeks later, she's already relayed this information to Gronw, and they've formed a cunning plan. So, he's sitting down to supper with Bloedwedd again, and she says, "Llewey..." and he says, "What?"

She says, "I'm still worried about this killing thing" so he says, "Why? It's so unlikely." Bloduedd looks at him coyly, and says, "I know it's unlikely, but I just can't... if I could just see." Llew says, "What do you mean?" and she responds, "well, I got the hang of the part where you can only be killed by a spear that has been carved over a year of Sundays." (Of course, secretly that's what Gronw had been doing for a year) "But the other stuff, it just doesn't make any sense. Could you perhaps show me."

With a sigh, Llew says, "Alright, just for you. I will show you." So, he called a servant, got him to set things up, and they basically put a large caldron under a roof with no walls, and they pulled a goat and tethered it next to the cauldron, and he stood with one foot on the goat, one foot on the rim of the caldron, under a roof without walls. And he says, "There you go. This is the only position..." (Thwunk!)

That's where the spear hit him. And of course, being a deity, being killed wasn't the end of the story for him. He transformed into an eagle and flew off into the air, flew off into the forest and eventually came to light on the top of the tallest tree in the forest.

Gwydion, at this point, comes back into the story, and he comes looking for Llew. He actually takes a sow with him to go hunting for Llew, and as they're going along, he... No, actually that's not quite right. He finds the sow at the bottom of the tree eating flesh that's falling down from above, and when he looks up, he sees this eagle pecking at its chest, and he realizes that this is Llew.

So he calls him down the tree and returns him to his normal form, and they go back. They have their revenge against Gronw by placing him the same position, but facing the other way and throwing the spear at him. Gronw asks, because Llew is such a powerful hunter, that he be allowed at least a small chance of surviving by having a standing stone between him and Llew. Of course, Llew throws the spear and it goes right through the stone and into Gronw, and that's the end of that.

So, that's the story of Llew. And for Lughnasadh, or for Lammas tide, the key part of that whole point from where Llew stands on the cauldron and the goat, and gets killed by the spear of Gronw, and the whole eagle and tree part, this is all very relevant to the time of year. We'll take a look at that in a moment , but first, I'm actually going to share a song with you that I wrote a couple of years ago. This is called "On the Balance". And it's an interesting take on the story of Llew.

On the Balance

1
The challenges have been met
And in timely frame
The first time you showed your skill
The day you earned your name

2
She told you you would be nameless
Your name was hers to give

A gift she would never offer
As long as she did live

Chorus
But you were led by the hand of the trickster
On the balance you did stand
Your adventures a perilous journey
The path from boyhood to the man

Refrain
She couldn't stop you
From taking what was yours
She could only make you earn it
The eagle in you soars...

3
The illusion of battle caused her
To place weapons in your hand
You took hold of your own manhood
The master of your Land

4
But there was still something missing
What you needed was a wife
The Trickster was there to help you
It would only cost your life

Chorus

Refrain
Innocence is no shield
For the hunter's guile
She sought out your deadly secret
With a simple smile
5
You stood on the cauldron, balanced

As the hunter took his shot
The sound of your body falling
Though your spirit was not

6
Flying across the treetops
Till the Trickster brought you down
Now that you are immortal
You wear your father's crown

Refrain
Ignorance is no defense
The hunter met his fate
You sought for poetic justice
For the lover of your mate

Chorus
The Trickster led you true
To the person that you must be
On the balance is where I find you
Where you truly set me free.

(© 2003 Peter Paddon)

So, the whole thing is about the sacred king cycle for me personally. I really don't pay a lot of attention to the agricultural cycle anymore, because I just get so focused on the whole Sacred King thing.

In that respect, midsummer sacrifice and the sacrifice at Lammas is sort of combined. The first sacrifice at midsummer is, of course, where the Sacred King, the chosen one who hasn't really come into his kingship yet, is sacrificing or giving up his freewill, his choice to do as he pleases.

If you like, at Beltane, it's the time of the coming of age and sowing of the wild oats and having a damn fine bit of fun, as it were. Then

140

at Midsummer, it's putting away your own desires and taking upon yourself the needs of the tribe or the clan or the family or the coven and putting those first. So you cease to be your own person. You become that servant of the land, if you like, that true kingship is, which is symbolized at Midsummer by the lobbing of the mistletoe or the symbolic castration of the Sacred King.

Luckily for us, castration of deities seems to be a temporary measure rather than a permanent one, otherwise we'd have run out of deities a long time ago and they wouldn't come to our parties either. So that's the sacrifice at Midsummer, the Sacrifice of Desire, to make room for what must be. And then at Lammas, the sacrifice is the sacrifice of the Sacred King himself, potentially.

We obviously hope that isn't the case, and so we prepare a scapegoat and hope that the Gods take the scapegoat. Now this may sound like a very trite, sort of silly game that we're talking about. But I guess you have to go through it, really, to actually feel just how real it becomes. You really do feel that the life of the Sacred King is in the balance, and that they may not come back from this experience. If they don't feel that way, if you don't fee that way, then you're not doing it right.

So the Lammas sacrifice is the sacrifice of the life of the King or the Scapegoat. And for us, we make life fairly simple by having a bread man as our scapegoat. It's a lot easier to explain to the police, for one thing, plus it's tasty when we get to eat it. And 99.9 times out of 100 the scapegoat is a suitable sacrifice, and we make damn sure it is anyway by putting a lot of juju into it to make it a worthy sacrifice.

It has been known in the path we walk for the Sacred King to be taken. Although to be honest, it was a case of somebody who knew their time was up. They were extremely ill, and they chose to be Sacred King to make something of value out of their passing. If we have a Sacred King who is taken around Lammas tide, it

141

doesn't have to be actually in the ritual. It can happen anytime after Midsummer. But the moment, if the Sacred King dies for real, then we go straight into dark time.

It's like Hallowe'en happens early for us, because we see the Sacred King as going into the mound at Samhain, and so we don't call on any male deity in a direct way, we don't do any aspecting or possession work with male deities during the dark time for that reason, because we see them all as being busy in the mound. So, it does an interesting thing to our wheel. It's only happened once that I'm aware of, and it was quite profound, so I'm told - I wasn't around for that one.

So we all absolutely hope that the scapegoat is a suitable sacrifice when we do this, and we basically hang on the world tree. We use our stang as a Bile Tree in the center of the circle, and we all hang on it by a cord, those of us who are initiates. We descend the Tree.

We descend to the Underworld with the Sacred King and the scapegoat. Hopefully we all come back up, and the scapegoat gets ripped into pieces and shared between those who hanged on the tree. I can't really say too much more about the hanging on the tree part - not because it's some deep dark secret, it's just that having hung on the tree in several roles, as Sacred King, as plain old initiate, and as Gronw taking everybody down, it is just an experience that defies words really. It is an incredible experience.

Doing it as Sacred King is something that you really only ever want to do once in your life. But you really, really, really don't want to miss doing it that one time. It's really quite awe inspiring. And so we hang on the tree. We descend to the underworld. We encounter various things to do with our tradition down there. And we find our way back up again. Meanwhile, the rest of the coven is milling like crazy. First to get help us down there, and then they change direction on the mill to pull us back up again. And it is a very profound, very emotional experience for everyone concerned, hanging on the tree and milling. It's one of the most potent rituals we do in the year. And it's also, I think pretty much unanimously amongst our initiates, it's pretty much our favorite ritual as well, because it's so intense and so visceral.

There I used that word again. Somebody in one of the forums was mentioning about me talking about the visceral experience of this path, and Lammas is definitely a time when you feel that as strong as strong can be. See, hopefully you've guessed by now that when Llew gets speared and he flies off as an eagle and then at the top of the tree, he's basically in the position of the king waiting to die. He's this incomplete spirit, he's falling apart, he's beginning to break down into the components of life, to cease to be in fact. And he's up there on the tallest tree in the forest, which is a very good metaphor the Bilé Tree, for the World Tree.

It is Gwydion the trickster who coaxes him down the tree, back down to the Underworld, to the place of the sow Ceridwen, where she's eating the pieces of flesh that are falling off - the rotting flesh. In a way she does that to recycle them and to help restore him.

Finally, having descended the tree, he is able to resume his shape as a man, as a king, as the Sacred King, and take his mantle upon him as an immortal, as a force within his realm. So this is very, very important, and there are of course layers and layers. I'm giving you a very very simple basics of it, in the hopes that you will think about it, meditate on it, and explore it yourself and find some of the deeper ramifications of this whole process. It is very profound.

It's one of the most sacred moments for me, for any witch in my opinion. And there are just so many levels and so many depths to it that I can't stress enough how much this is a very important part of the Wheel, as far as I'm concerned, at least in the path I walk. If you don't walk the Sacred King cycle, you might not agree with me - and that's fine too. I mean, were not talking about a one true

143

right and only way here. We're talking about this is the way that we do things. And maybe it resonates with you, maybe it doesn't.

But even if doesn't resonate with you, it might help you think about something else that does resonate with you, and so it may be of value to you, and that's why I'm sharing it. Anyway, that's pretty much it for this week. I hope you've enjoyed it.

Traditions of Witchcraft

Episode 27, broadcast on August 22, 2006

Welcome to the Crooked Path. My name is Peter Paddon and this week, I'm taking a long hard look at traditions. We'll take a look at red threads and white, the latter being a variation on silver thread term used by Robin Artisson in some of his articles. I just prefer white to silver.

First of all, let's take a look at red threads. There are traditions all over the place, traditional witches, traditional druids, traditional crafters, cunning folk, and one of the things they have in common is that if they are claiming to be pre-Gardnerian, they tend to make a big deal about having some sort of lineage going back at least a couple of generations.

And some claim a lineage that goes back millennia. I'm not at the moment going to comment on the validity of those, but there is a very strong need it seems for people to prove that they have a real lineage, and so you get a lot of claims that cannot really be proven. They're either taken at face value or they're disputed.

A lot of the battling between different covens, different traditions, tends to be over their claims of lineage. "Well, they say this, but they're not really." It seems to be an endless sort of entertainment for those of us who don't want to get involved in that sort of discussion.

Watching these people battling it out on whose tradition is more real and lineaged than whose. It really does beg the question, are there really any real old traditions out there? And I have to say, on the face of the evidence, I don't think there are. I don't think there is any tradition in existence today that has an unbroken lineage going back more than two or three generations, because there's just no evidence to support it. It's really quite sad that people keep

145

trying to insist there are, because it's not like it makes you any less of a witch if you haven't got that.

So what does make a tradition traditional? Heh, Heh. There's a question. Basically, a tradition is a coherent body of lore and practice that is taken and passed on from teacher to student. That's what makes a tradition. You don't have to have the blood oath pact made with your grandmother. You don't have to have the ancient scratchy writings from fourteen generations back. A tradition becomes a tradition when it is passed from a teacher to a student and is a coherent body of work. That's all there is to it, nothing more really. And the insistence on trying to prove lineage to other people is basically down to a lack of self confidence, I think, because the whole idea of "I discovered this while was daydreaming one day, and it works really well. Here, try it." just doesn't sound as convincing, I guess, as "This has been passed down through all the generations of our tradition from the days when before the Christians came."

You see what I mean? There's this sort of air of nobility, I guess, that having one of these fabled lineages gives you. Now, to be fair, you know the whole thing was set in motion probably by Samual Liddell "MacGregor" Mathers, one of the founders of the Hermetic Order of the Golden Dawn, who did an incredible job of taking western hermeticism, alchemy, cabala, and various other brands of magic, ceremonial magic, and synthesizing them into a cohesive whole. He forged a tradition out of all these disparate elements. It is absolutely amazing. The Golden Dawn is the premiere magical order of the western world. It has more influence and has influenced more people and more organizations than any other body of initiates in the history of western civilization. So that's quite an accomplishment that they did, back towards the end of the nineteenth century.

But that wasn't enough. For some reason, they had to turn around and forge documents to prove that they had received this tradition from this ancient secret society. And that's really what got the ball rolling. It was all downhill from there, because everybody who came after had to prove that they had been around a lot longer than they really had. The Bavarian Illuminati who are invoked in modern myth as the great conspirators, were in reality a quasi-Masonic secret society that created a fake history for itself.

Everybody does it. Gerald Gardener comes along and puts together a really quite worth while tradition which came to be known as Gardnerian Wicca, and added lineage to it, that it came from the back of beyond . It's like they were afraid that it wouldn't stand up on its own merits.

And this continues today. So people come across something, and they actually make something that is quite special, and then they turn around and say, "Oh, I got this from the ancients of such and such," or "my grandmother passed this on. It's been in our family for generations," or "this is based upon work that I did with my great aunt when I was a school child," and so on and so forth.

What you end up with is this web of deceit that is quite unnecessary, but get's so embedded into the tradition that nobody dare strip it away for fear of destroying the tradition itself.

There's a big deal made by some people about Witch Blood as well. Witch blood is the concept, usually based on the legends of the Watchers or the Annunaki, to use the Sumerian original version of the myth, where the angelic beings came down and bred with humans to create this race of Watchers, this race of quasi-divine beings who are the originators of the Witch Blood line, the Sacred King line as well for that matter. And whether you believe that or not is neither here nor there.

Often there are traditions that use the concept of Witch Blood to limit who they allow in and out. They basically look to see that you have the signs of having the Witch Blood. Now given the way genetics works, and the way that it's actually been fairly substantially proven that the entire human race can be traced back to six or seven individuals due to the human race having a radical decrease in size early in its history, genetically speaking, if the story of Witch Blood and the Annunaki is true, we all have some. Everybody has Witch Blood.

So the real question is, that innate presence that is in everyone, has it been awakened? And this is the real difference. For me, I believe in the concept of Witch Blood, myself. Just so you know that I'm that kind of freak. But I believe that it's in everybody. And the difference is that in people who work the Craft and become real Witches, the latent something, X-factor or whatever you want to call it, has been awakened, because with it comes memories, ancestral memories.

And that really is the key to me, of a traditional Witch, is working with the ancestral memories, working with the ancestors and forging a link there. So Witch Blood is important, but it's important for everybody. I believe that if you could find a way to awaken everybody, everyone could be Witches. But I think there are people where it's buried too deeply, or they have too many other factors that prevent them from awakening, and so witchcraft isn't for them, basically.

The whole tradition thing, you know, whatever toots your horn. If you need to claim seventeen generations of lineage back to Argle Fargle, the high priest of Doobrey-Hicks, that's fine if it works for you. But don't expect me to bow down in awe when you tell me that, because even if it's absolutely true, it really has no bearing on me. I'm going to acknowledge your ability as a Witch based on what I see before me, not on your pedigree. So you know, it still boils down to you have to have it in you.

Ancestry, lineage, a venerable tradition is not going to make you a better witch - you make you a better witch. And so this whole concept of lineage, the red thread if you will, of lore and practice being passed down from generation to generation, teacher to student, yes it is valid, but is it really the only answer? Is it really the only thing that matters? The answer to that is a categorical no, it isn't. You can forge your own link and you can create something very valid without that. And we'll be talking about that next.

So what about the white thread? The white thread is much like the red thread except there's no tradition involved yet. The white thread is where you actually make direct link with the gods, with the ancestors, whatever you want to call them, and recover or create lore directly that way.

It's not as easy as being taught something by somebody who's already done it. But it is perfectly valid, and I would say ninety percent of the work that my group does, Briar Rose, is recovering lore or exploring lore that we have received directly from the ancestors. We started off being trained in particular techniques and we've moved on from that. We continue growing and learning, and our connections now are directly with our ancestors and our deities.

I think that even a red thread, even a tradition that does have lineage should be doing this sort of work, because that's how a tradition evolves and grows. If you're not doing that then you've become stagnant and dogmatic, you're not really going anywhere, and you're really wasting your time in my opinion. But I'm fairly opinionated.

Now I'm calling this the white thread, because I tend to like the symbolism of red and white as a polarity thing. Robin Artisson refers to it in his writings as silver thread, and he is probably the first person who's actually made a big deal out of actually working his craft as a silver thread or white thread. He makes no bones about the fact that he's not working on an ordained of old traditional system that's been passed down for generations. He's actually gone out there. He's learned from various people what he can. And then

149

he's taken it all and taken it into sacred space and worked it and forged his own relationship with his ancestors and his deities, and created a very sound tradition out of it.

Those of you who've read his book Witching Way of the Hollow Hill will know what I'm talking about. It's probably the best traditional craft book out there at the moment, because he doesn't make any claims of being initiated by grandparents or receiving mantles from mythical beings or so on and so forth. He's actually making a lot of waves through doing this, and hopefully it's the start of a movement where people begin to realize that they don't have to make these stupid claims of ancient lineage in order to be taken seriously.

I know it's certainly shaking up a lot of the people who have made claims of ancient lineage, and it's one of the reasons why I think people are so polarized either for or against Robin is because his stance makes them uncomfortable, because it shows them up to be idiots. And I'm sure you know a few people who fall into that category. The whole idea of white thread is to take whatever it is you have and create something new out of it. Start a new tradition if you like, and rather than base it upon what your grandmother may or may not have told you when she was washing your hair in the bathtub, it's something that you actually, you take your experiences of working with deity and you turn that into something valid and something real.

The key here really is going to the source instead of looking for people to show you the way, go to the ancestors. The ancestors are very close to the surface. All you have to do is open yourself up to them and you'll find them. They're quite literally in your blood, and the ancestral memories are in your blood.

For me, the ancestral memories are very similar in concept to Jung's idea of a collective unconscious, cellular memory, all those theories. I think it's just different ways of describing the same thing. We

150

have these memories within us. This is quite literally the Witch Blood, if you like. My favorite theory, and I have no way of knowing whether it's true, but fits the bill for me, so that's the one I use when I'm explaining things to myself or fooling myself, depending on how you look at it, is the idea that the so called junk DNA, the DNA that doesn't seem to do anything practical in our genetic makeup, actually somehow contains a matrix that stores these ancestral memories.

So they're there to be tapped into. And all you have to do is open yourself up and look within and without at the same time. It's another of those wonderful paradoxes I keep talking about. Tapping the bone, doing oracular work, opening yourself up to the ancients, this is all stuff that you can find techniques online for doing this. In Robin's books, you'll find techniques that work perfectly well for doing this, and also in the book that I'm working on at the moment -a quick plug - *A Grimoire for Modern Cunning Folk*[1]. But my book is going to be very much a practical manual on how to make these sort of links for yourself, because I believe that every tradition can be a valid tradition if you actually open yourself up to working and growing with the ancestors.

And so it's become my mission in life to encourage people to do just that. See, the trick is a lot of the "old" traditions... a lot of the traditional trads talk about being part of the River of Blood. The River of Blood is the flow of the ancestors, the initiates of old, if you like. You get this image of a torrent or current, and current is another name that's used for it. You get the impression that only they have swimming permits or something. But it's really not true.

In order to become a witch, you need to immerse yourself in the River of Blood. This is a term that is used traditionally quite a lot. And to be perfectly honest, that term means that you can step off the bank at any point and immerse yourself in the River of Blood,

1   To be published by Pendraig in October 2009

151

quite literally, quite simply. It helps if you have a buoyancy device in the form of some sort of connection with the ancestors. And so, it's not easy. It's not necessarily difficult in the technical sense. But it's not an easy thing to do, because you generally have to get out of your own way.

We tend to interfere with our own process by trying to analyze it. And the real key to working with the ancestors is being able to get yourself into that poetic space, that place where everything is now, and where the logic circuits are pretty much switched off, and then employ one of the many techniques that are available to make contact with the ancestors and with your patron deities, and so on and so forth.

And then, just listen to them. When they give you practical advice, try it and see. Don't take it as written. Don't take it as gospel, if you'll pardon the expression, but try it and see. Always have an open inquiring mind and try these things out. And you'll find that very soon you're starting to get a body of practice and lore that you're turning to again and again, because it works, pure and simply, not because somebody said it was great and authentic or anything like that, but because it works for you. And suddenly, you're building a cohesive practice. You have lore to back it up. You have a tradition in embryonic form.

And then one day, you find yourself passing it on to somebody else. You're facilitating them having the same experiences. You're helping them to explore and forge their own links with the ancestors, putting together some sort of rite of passage of initiation into the group. All of a sudden, guess what, your white thread has just turned red, because you've passed on your tradition to somebody else and you've started a new red thread tradition.

They all started that way somewhere, whether it was last week or three hundred years ago. And so, don't be afraid to let go and open up and drop all the pomp and ceremony of "oh, my tradition's been

152

around longer than yours." Look for the real thing that matters, and that's the link with the ancestors, the link with your patron deities. And just go for it. Make your own real connection. Make your tradition real. That's all that really matters.

And with careful reading of books that have been around for a long time, and taking books like Robin's books and hopefully my book when it comes out, you'll find that you too can create a real traditionm, and you don't need to rely on your grandmother to help you out.

The Mystery of Initiation

Episode 29, broadcast on September 4, 2006

Hello, and welcome to the Crooked Path. I'm Peter Paddon and this week I'm continuing a line of somewhat controversial topics by taking a look at initiation.

So initiation, what are we talking about when we use the term initiation? Now the word literally means a beginning, a start of something. And this is probably one of the biggest areas of contention because most people seem to work towards initiation as if it were a goal, it was the end of the journey, when in actual fact, it should be considered the first step on the journey.

We always tell our initiates, once they've been initiated, that now they really start to learn, because really everything leading up to that point was just preparing them for the experience of initiation. Of course, there are several different things that come under the category of initiation when we're talking about magical groups, and we're going to start off by taking a look at the initiation ritual as a rite of passage.

Initiation into the group, this is often a very key moment in anybody's studies, because it's the point at which you cease to be a 'maybe' member of the group and become an actual member of the group. It's the point at which you start to really start learning the inner workings of the tradition that you're studying, and so this is very very key, but does it have any significance beyond that?

Well, for starters it is a rite of passage, and rites of passage for many reasons, psychological, social, even physiological in some respects can have quite a profound effect on us. Other rites of passage are... of course, there's the ultimate rites of passage of birth and death, which are really take you from one world into another in a very literal way.

155

And then there's the naming rite, by whatever name your spiritual path uses, Christening, Wiccaning, so on and so forth. The rite of adulthood, of coming of age. A wedding is a rite of passage into a new state of existence as part of a couple, and divorce as well can be a rite of passage, especially if you have a nasty one.

But all these rites of passage come from community life, and they tend to have a very profound affect on us psychologically. A rite of initiation into a group, a magical group, coven, whatever you want to call it, is no less profound in a psychological sense, because it is a sort of coming of age, becoming a valid member of society type thing within this very specialized group. You're no longer seen as children. You're seen people who are responsible and ready to learn the secrets, if you like.

It all sounds very mysterious, learning deep dark secrets of the tradition, and it usually turns out to be a little disappointing if you think about it in that sense. Remember one of the great quotes about Aleister Crowley was how he, at his Golden Dawn initiation, swore these huge oaths of secrecy, never to reveal what was given to him within the confines of the temple, and they then presented to him the great secret of the Hebrew alphabet, which he wasn't overly impressed with.

This is one of the issues that a lot of groups come up against time and time again, this anticlimactic nature of some of the rituals. My own experience, having been something of a initiation whore, I've joined lots of different groups over the years, ceremonial magic, Wiccan, traditional witchcraft, and one of the things a lot of them have in common is that the initiation ritual starts out as being this mysterious thing that "how am I going to survive it?" and by the end of it, you're sort of "oh, will it please end before I die of boredom?"

Especially in ceremonial groups, the symbolism is laid on so thick that it obscures any real sort of participation on the part of the initiate. The candidate is moved from point to point and has symbol after symbol thrown at them, and it all becomes a meaningless daze after a while. You have to wonder whether there was really any point to it in the first place by the time you get to the end. A lot of the ceremonial groups follow the format of Masonic initiations which are big on symbolism.

Of course, one of the advantages the Masons have is that their initiation has a few very key points to it that makes it very effective psychologically, and unfortunately, they tend to be the things that get left out by magical groups. So you end up with the words and the movements and the symbolism, and it can be very moving, but there's always that danger of slipping into role playing, which really doesn't do a lot of good.

And when you rely on a symbolic initiation ritual, there is always that danger, because there isn't really any way you can fail initiations based on symbolism, unless there's a test, and very rarely is there a test that they're going to fail. So the most important thing about the rite of passage that is initiating into a group is the act of joining the family or the tradition. Whilst this can be a very magically effective experience as I'll discuss shortly, for the most part it tends to be something along the lines of fraternity initiations, often complete with hazing and joshing about and trying to terrify the poor candidate beforehand as well. You know, that's a find old tradition too, but it's not really an essential part of the experience.

Now sometimes groups do do something a bit more profound, and most often the most profound initiations, rites of passage into a group, are the ones where there is some reciprocal accepting going on. It's not just the person being inducted into the group, but the group being wrapped around the person. And the most significant of all is where there is some sort of claiming of the candidate by the group, and this is often done in traditional witchcraft, it's often the ancestors that do the claiming in some from or other.

157

Many of the groups that refer to themselves as family traditions or even just traditional witchcraft groups these days, will tend to have a two tier sort of passage of entry. The first is a rite of fostering, where you get to become a formal student. You're an initiate student, but you're not full family, you've been fostered rather than made a member of the family.

Then later on there is a rite of adoption, which is the being claimed by the ancestors and the gods of the tradition. And this can be very very profound, both on the psychological level and also on the magical level. This is where it starts to get really interesting. It's one of the things that we do in our own group. I mean, I don't think there's any secrets being given away, because there isn't really any secret to it. We have that two tier approach and it's not so much a case of somebody being more important or more in the group if they've taking the second part of the thing. It's just a matter of you get initiated into our group, you get fostered in and you become a crafter, and at some point you reach a level of experience and hunger as much as anything else that you decide to take that next step and that next step is to go through a process where you are claimed by the ancestors. And it's a very simple, they either claim you or they don't. It's very unambiguous. And it's been very effective for us.

And there's no pomp and circumstance with us. We don't do big drawn out rituals for this. It's just a particular experience that either does or does not succeed for you. And that's it, end of story. The first initiation is very big on some other aspects, and I'll be talking about some of that later, because that ties in more with the inner initiation, which is the other side of the coin, and which is really the most important one.

So, the rite of passage into the group is very important psychologically as a way of making you feel like you belong to the group and feel united and an integral part of it and very much important. The traditional witch is the aspect of being claimed by the tradition, by the ancestors, but the ultimate initiatory experience is one that cannot be given to you by any tradition. It may occur within the practices of a tradition, but ultimately it occurs within you. And this is the personal inner initiation.

So the real initiation, which comes from within, it's the initiation that we're all talking about when we actually talk about initiation, it's the big one. It is the direct experience between you and your path, your spirituality, your deities, however you want express it, but the most important thing is that it comes from within and it comes from you. There's nobody that can give it to you or bestow it upon you or make it happen for you.

In an ideal situation, a teacher or a group that you're working with will provide you with experiences that will facilitate the development of a state of existence within you where you can encounter the true initiation, and if you're really lucky, this will coincide with some sort of rite of passage initiatory experience within the group. That's what we usually try to aim for in my group, is to try and get the candidate into a position where they're ripe for a real initiatory experience about the same time as when we do the rite of initiation into the group, so that the two more or less overlap and they can have a very profound interaction with each other in that way.

But there's no guarantees, and they don't have to coincide to be effective, each in their own sphere of existence. As I said, the most important thing to bear in mind is that this initiation comes from within you. So it's not something that is a gift given by anybody else. It's not going to be something that happens without you putting some effort into it, because it is very very dependent on you actually being ready for it, and this is what a lot of the training in a good group is all about, is giving you the tools and giving you the experiences to get yourself into a place where you can enter that fulcrum point at the heart of the compass where everything is now and everything is one, where you can encounter the experiences that transform you.

159

This is what initiation is about. It's about inner transformation. Once you've experienced an inner initiation, you will never be the same again, and this is probably one of the biggest differences between the group initiation and the inner initiation, is that you can leave a group but you can never walk away from an initiation that happened at an inner level. It's part and parcel of you. It's literally part of your DNA. There's no going back, no turning back the clock to before it, and this can be enough reason for people to say, "No, I'm done." They catch a glimpse of what's around the corner, realize that if they take that extra step, that what they're glimpsing is going to be part and parcel of their lives from there onwards, and they decide not to take that step. That is a perfectly valid choice to make, and that is in and of itself a form of initiation, although it's an initiation into a more mundane way of being, because you've turned away from what might have been.

And you know, they're not always easy. There are... you know it's not like there's just one big one. There are a series of these that go on for the rest of your life essentially. But the important thing here, I think, is that you very much get a hunger for this, and it's the needing to step forward into that darkness and accept the experience for what it is that makes it a very profound experience for you. As I said, that once you've taken that step there is no going back, and it does tend to change your life in every aspect. The mundane, the spiritual, your interactions with other people, it does tend to have very profound effects, and people do notice.

We talk about the Witch's Mark or the Mark of Cain, which is the mark of the initiate, and some groups actually physically mark their initiates and some groups don't, but everyone who undergoes one of these inner initiations is marked in a way that is very clear to others who have also been through these experiences. You can always tell another initiate without being told, because you can see the scars if you like of that initiation upon their psyche. You can see the mark on their aura.

160

You can see, you can just tell, because something in you resonates with them and you realize that you are talking to a kindred spirit. And that is really quite an amazing thing when you get that. When you get a group that is very good at bringing people to these points of inner initiation, and so that you have the majority of the members of the group do actually undergo these inner initiations, they tend to become very close knit.

They tend to become very very good at communicating with each other about these things, which is in itself very rare, because communicating these inner experiences is very difficult, because finding words for it is very hard. But when you're speaking to someone who's already been through it, you find you can communicate it better, because the few words that are available tend to work that much more effectively. You tend to end up with, "You remember when you do that?", "Oh yeah yeah, I remember that." You get conversations like that. It doesn't sound like much in the way of communication, but because you've been through that shared experience, it's enough. It's enough to trigger what you're getting, what you're trying to get across, and this is really quite a profound part of the bond that initiates share.

It's a very powerful compensation for the other part of the... you know... the curse, if you like, of the inner initiation, which is the isolation that it places upon you, because these initiations, these inner initiations are very personal and very intimate. They're also very isolating. I talked in the pilot episode of this podcast about the terrible loneliness of the initiate, the sense of wandering in the wasteland alone, even when you're part of a group. You get these very profound moments of realizing that though you walk alongside others, you are in fact isolated and completely alone, and this can be very difficult to deal with.

It's one of the things that people can shy away from, and that prevents people from going further into the mysteries. But that is as it should be, because it's not meant to be for everybody to walk

161

through these mysteries. It's meant for the few people to take the road less traveled and to do what they can to grow spiritually and promote themselves through these experiences in the hopes that by doing so they gradually help the human race to do the same, by pulling itself up by its own bootstraps.

This has often been described as the great work. It's the idea of the individual striving for their own personal spiritual evolution, by doing so helps to raise the evolutionary state of the entire human race. And so, whether we like it or not, the human race as a whole gradually becomes more spiritual. Despite the evidence to the contrary that we see in the world around us, there is evidence to suggest that the human race is becoming more spiritual.

Part of the process is becoming more self aware, and this is the status that we find ourselves in now where the... this going to sound terribly old fashioned and I apologize if it offends anyone, but I'm just putting forward a theoretical principle here, the idea that historically the human race has not been really known for individuality. In medieval times the feudal mindset was the way things went, and everybody worked together in a sort of communal way. Individuality was not rewarded and not expected.

As time has passed by, the great individuals have cropped up, individual thinkers like Galileo and Newton and so on and so forth, all great thinkers and philosophers and inventors and scientists, and gradually the concept of individuality has become more of a reality for the human race. Now what we find is that the western world has become very self absorbed, because we've become very aware of ourselves, and we're going through a phase that is akin to the teenage years, I guess, in human terms, because we've become self aware and so self is all we are aware of at the moment.

The third world countries, some of them have retained that group mentality for longer. And so they're starting to develop this self awareness and they're starting to make a little noise about that.

And so what you see is an interesting mix in the world now, where the various states of spiritual evolution are coming into conflict, because everything has its native aspects.

You sort of go through a negative process when you achieve self awareness, because you become self absorbed, you become very childish and selfish and wanting everything for yourself, and it takes a little while for that to settle in and for you to start to actually look at things from a wider perspective and let the self awareness stop being a negative and start being positive thing, enables you to actually operate for the greater good. So I think there's a lot of promise for the human race as long as we keep on evolving spiritually.

If we were to get stuck where we are now, it would be a disaster, but hopefully we'll find the next step forward collectively as a species before we totally obliterate ourselves. Heh, heh. There's always hope.

pitfalls on the path

Episode 38, broadcast on November 20, 2006

Hello and welcome to the crooked path I am Peter Paddon, and we were going to have a round table on finding your path this week. But due to timing issues, that's had to be postponed, and instead I'm going to take a look at the pitfalls on the path.

Now it won't come as any surprise to you that the Crooked Path is not an easy path. Its not for nothing that it often described as the road less traveled, and there are indeed a lot of pitfalls for the unwary in following the path, and even those who consider themselves quite experienced can encounter some of these pitfalls and fall into them if you will.

So it doesn't hurt to have a reminder every now and then of just exactly what sort of dangers your placing yourself in, and I don't mean in the sense of booby traps and wild animals kind of danger. But the danger of looking stupid, or even worse being stupid, and the danger of derailing your path or getting yourself in such a pickle that you actually step away from your path and fail to achieve your goals and your Fate. Theres a lot to say that you can't not achieve your Fate, but you can certainly derail your process and make it more difficult for yourself.

So, lets start off by having a look at some of the personal pitfalls, some of the things that you can do for or to yourself on this path to make life difficult. The first one is pretty much unavoidable - we all go through this at the beginning, its being too green to know any better. One of the real skills that you develop when your walking the crooked path is the skill of discernment, being able to basically recognize what's crap and what isn't, and right at the beginning that's not a skill that we are inherently born with.

You can maybe smell the BS if your lucky and you have good intuition, but you're never really going to know for sure, you have to take at least some of it on trust until you find out, and the only way out of this pitfall is experience... if you step in poop often enough you're going to learn to recognise it from a distance and avoid it, its as simple as that and we've all done it.

We've all been all wide eyed and innocent and taken something as gospel that was poked at us in fun; it's not unknown for even the best of teachers to play games with their students and to have a little bit of a laugh at their expense sometimes.

I myself have been guilty of that particular pleasure. I remember one year my pre-iniate class back home in England, the class had fell on April 1st which should have been a big red flag for the students, but apparently wasn't, and so I proceeded to teach them a class, spent the entire evening teaching them a class on this south American magical system complete with Chakra colours and quarter callings and words of power and all sorts of stuff like that, and even went so far as getting them to construct a ritual using this system at the end of the evening.

It wasn't until after that I proceeded to explain to them how all of the words of power were terms from the game of pool or snooker pronounced backwards, the chakra colors where the colors of the balls on the snooker table and the whole thing was a complete fabrication - however they managed to raise some interesting energy doing it so I guess if you believe in what your doing it doesn't really matter about the details so much, to a certain extent. But I lost a student out of that, an older woman who got in a huff because her time had been wasted, it was April 1st, but never mind. Its not something I have repeated since because I've never had a class that fell on April 1st since then, so who knows what might happen if I have another one in the future. But anyway it was a good laugh for 99 percent of the people involved, one person got in a bit of a huff, she actually got more in a huff because I put one of the younger

166

students centering the circle and she felt that was inappropriate because he was young and she basically thought that she should be doing it and she didn't have that much ability or knowledge, to be honest and was no great loss, so I wasn't at all upset to see her go. So, thats "too green to know any better".

There is also "too trusting to be discerning". This is more of a pitfall when you have a teacher than when you are a solitary explorer on this particular path. The assumption that everything that comes from your teachers mouth is a golden gem, that is to be treasured and nurtured and taken at face value, because your teacher is all knowing and superhuman. We've all been there too, and we've all been rudely awakened because there's no such thing as the all-seeing all-wise teacher.

Usually, in fact invariably, teachers are as fallible and as struggling as the rest of us, they're just maybe a few steps further up the mountain than we are, and so you have to learn to be discerning about what you're being taught. Anyone who expects blind faith from you isn't doing you a favor, because this path isn't a path of faith, its a path of gnosis - that means knowledge, and the way you turn what you're being taught into gnosis is by making it yours.

You take it in, and you examine it, and you evaluate it, and you make it yours. Its the whole process of synthesis that I talked about last week - you can't just take something as gospel, you have to make it yours, you have to make sure that it actually is true for you and so this is a very important part of the process.

On the flipside of that, you get the student who is too cynical to experience the wonder of this path. This can be just as difficult as someone is too trusting because someone who is too trusting never really takes ownership of stuff which is the biggest deal, but they also never stop to check whether what they are being taught is actually genuine and that can be a pitfall of one kind, but being too cynical is really a flipside, you get this a lot from people who came into this path from a stance of atheism or from a very intellectual background, they kind of feel that this is right, but there is a part of them that still says "no this is a load of crap".

They really want to be convinced of everything, they want proof and that in itself isn't a bad thing, its just that its when it gets to the point that you're too cynical to allow the possibility, too cynical to give it a chance to succeed or fail, thats when the problem arises.

Then of course you always get the people who are just too lazy to do anything, if you fall into that category theres really no hope for you because only you can solve that problem. There's a lot of people who are very enthusiastic about their path, whether its traditional witchcraft or Wicca or Odinism or Asatru or whatever, and they will happily turn up for every circle, they will turn up for every class, but when you ask them what they have done in between them they go "huh? I had to do something?" It doesn't occur to them to actually study or research, or even practice by themselves, and they really get out of it what they put into it. Then it becomes more like a social event, which is a real pity because usually it doesn't take a lot of effort to actually start to get results, and once you start getting results you tend to be a little less inclined to be lazy, because you get hungry for it.

Of course the biggest personal pitfall, and the biggest annoyance as far as I'm concerned personally - it is a personal peeve - is allowing yourself to become an armchair occultist. This is where you've read the books, you can quote the rituals, you can quote Crowley and Regardie and Cochrane and Gardner and Sanders and Robin Artisson, and you can describe exactly how to draw a perfect pentagram in the Golden Dawn system, and you can correct people on their pronunciation of Enochian. But you've never actually done anything, because its all reading, book learning, and sitting in an armchair pontificating about it, and reading more books about it.

The majority of so-called ceremonial magicians fall into this category, for probably ninety percent of ceremonial magicians actually are armchair occultists who may have gone to the effort of buying some of the ritual tools, and theres only that small core, that ten percent, that actually work the systems. I think you're less likely to become an armchair occultist in traditional witchcraft, because there isn't so much to memorize, because you tend to have to work from the heart rather than from a script, and I think traditional witchcraft tends to appeal more to people who actually do things than want to sit around being academic about it. So thats a couple of the pitfalls that you can actually set out as traps for yourself. Next, we'll take a look at some of the pitfalls that can be thrown at you from other people.

So when it comes to pitfalls that have been left lying around for you on this path by other people, it really does become important to be able to have that sense of discernment, knowing what is good and bad, and that does just come by experience. Of course, there are a couple of things that can help you when it comes to the external pitfalls.

Obviously the first pitfall you're going to find is good and bad books, and bad books tend to be fairly easy to spot, even to a reasonably novice person - if they have any common sense that is. So you can actually use common sense as a stand-in for experience to a certain extent when it comes to books.

Bad books, well luckily a lot of bad books all come from one publisher, Llewelyn. When it comes to traditional witchcraft they have almost nothing that is of value and their books tend to fall into the category that I like to describe as the "instant adept" syndrome, where they are saying "buy this book, and by the end of the week you will be a master of Enochian magic" or so on and so forth, and its really quite sad, because they might actually have started out as good books, but they get marketed so terribly - and Llewelyn interfere with them so much - that what could have been a good book becomes a very dubious book, and the main thing to take into account is that, when it comes to a publisher like Llewelyn, they (the publisher) are more important than the content of the book.

Unfortunately this is a trend that is getting more and more common in traditional publishing, which is why a lot of authors are starting to self publish, so they can actually have the control they feel they need to write the book they want, rather than the book the publishers think will sell lots of copies, and the thing to look out for with a bookis, is there anything that says this is easy, that you can learn it in a weekend or learn it very quickly or anything that smacks of "say this spell and it will work".

There is a very good example, I think, of the sort of person who believes these claims: on amazon.com there is a review for one of my spellcrafting DVD's - the Craftwise series. The very first one, volume one, which is about candle magic:

> " Its a very good DVD for beginners, but for people more experienced its not so good, because there are only three spells on the DVD and there is an awful lot of talking."

The DVD runs for about an hour and a half, and there is a lot of talking. In the class I talk an awful lot about how to create your own spells, and this person who has written a review has fallen into the trap of magic being a process of collecting spells, which is a very "Llewelyn" point of view, and has totally missed the fact that all that talking on the DVD is actually telling people how to create their own magic.

But then, that is one of the beauties of pitfalls... it stops idiots from having access to the good stuff, because they really don't pay attention, they miss out on it. Which is one of the reasons that I believe in the concept of hiding the secrets in plain sight, because if you are meant to know them, if you are at that point where they are right for you, then you will notice them - and if that isn't the case, then you won't notice them. Its as simple as that.

Then of course the other main source of external pitfalls on this path are from terrible teachers, and terrible teachers come in many different flavors, and even the best teachers are going to have some bad aspects because nobody is perfect - everyone is human. Everyone has flaws, and so the best of teachers are going to have some bad points, and what is really the difference between a good teacher and a bad teacher is, do their flaws interfere with the teaching process, or can you work with them? Can you work around it, it's as simple as that.

And so some teachers that might be good for one person are bad for another. I tend to work well with people who are interactive - I don't work well with people who give out photocopied notes every week. But other people do, so for them that person would be a good teacher, for me not so good. So there is a certain amount of subjectivity there, but there are certain flavors of teachers who are universally bad, and I want to just look at a couple of them.

The first one is probably the most obvious one, and thats people who actually don't have anything to teach, but their ego and their desire for power and influence has made them declare themselves to be a teacher. This happens more in the pagan community than it does anywhere else, I think, because there are no standards.

That sounds really bad, but what I mean is in most of the Christian denominations you have to get certain qualifications you have to have accredited documents to say that you actually know what you are talking about even if you don't, but you have to have the paperwork, I'm not saying that would be a good thing in paganism, I personally don't agree with it for pagans, certainly not our kind of pagans, but it does leave us open to people who have read a coffee table book and have decided they are the great high priest, or high priestess mucky muck, and they are going to teach the world how to do it right. You only have to read some of the comments from certain people on WitchVox, on the news articles to see that in action on a daily basis.

Pretty much anyone on WitchVox who is posting a comment to every single news article, every single day - theres a good chance that they fall into that category, theres a few certain people, I'm not going to name them for reasons of libel but I'm sure any of you who go there know who I am talking about, who have got an opinion on everything and know absolutely bugger all. And its all just a matter of ego feeding.

These people tend to be very egotistical, very controlling. But they are big and loud, and shiny and bright, in a wasteland of people hungry for learning and so they tend to get rather large groups gathered around them.

Next in line are those do have something to teach but they have a very similar ego problem, and they don't really want to share what they know for fear that you may go off and become better than them. So they do everything they can to demonstrate how knowledgeable and wise they are, without actually imparting any of that wisdom and knowledge to their students. That can get very frustrating if you are like me, you last about three classes in that, and then you say "screw this, I'm off to somebody who actually knows how to teach".

Then of course theres the kind of teacher who may or may not have stuff to teach, but they work on a principle... well, their motto might as well be "so what have you done for me lately?" People don't generally charge for training in traditional witchcraft, or even Wicca, because its generally seen as being against the rules, but there are ways to extract payment in other forms, like getting students to do your housework, getting them to drive you around like your own personal chauffeur service, or lending you money that you conveniently forget to pay back, and stuff like that - running errands, being an unpaid servant basically.

I believe there is a certain amount of service that is acceptable to be rendered to a teacher, they're taking their time out to share what they have with you, and so you should be a sharing person and should help out to a reasonable extent. But when you find yourself spending ninety percent of your time with them, doing stuff for them, and less than ten percent of your time actually learning anything, then there's probably something wrong with that equation.

Then theres possibly the worst kind of teacher of all, these are the teachers that actually have the knowledge and wisdom and are very good at sharing it, very good at teaching, they're very good at getting you to take ownership of the lore and become practiced at the practice, if you will pardon the expression. But the thing that they are not very good at is being honest about where it all came from. These are people, who maybe have self esteem issues, they feel the need to make themselves out to be more than they are, and so they've learned things from books or from talking with people ,but they have to pass it off as being some great ancient lineage that they are the latest adept in the line of.

Its really quite sad, because what they have to offer is generally very, very valid, and very useful, and they are good teachers. It is just that they have to falsify where it comes from in order to make themselves seem more important, or because they feel that if they said "well I got this from a book and I tweaked it around a bit and found a way of making it work better, but thats all it is" they feel that you won't accept it as being genuine, because its not from some grand old secret tradition, and that is really sad and pathetic.

Quite often you find that the same person will also have this other trait, which is the joint first in the label of absolute worst type of teacher. This is where these really good teachers really train you well ,but when the time comes for the parting of the ways, they can't let go of you. Now there are a million different reasons why a student and teacher may part company, inevitably it is going to happen at some point for some reason or another, and it is very important to bear in mind, because even in the most close-knit coven the people within that coven are basically a group of individuals whose paths happen for the time being to be going in the same direction.

But they will diverge sooner or later, and so people go off on their merry way, so you can't expect that people will be together forever, its not a life long commitment. Even though frequently the oaths and the initiation rituals make it out to be such. Its simply a matter of 'this is the path of the exile, the path of the outcast' and so even when you are part of a group or part of a tradition, you are still walking your own personal path that happens to coincide with that group or tradition for the time being, and so any teacher should be able to let go of their student for whatever reason.

If the student has decided to leave, there is no reason not to let them go amicably, because you can't stop them anyway. In this day and age there are laws against keeping people against their will, its called kidnap, its called unlawful arrest, its called all sorts of nasty horrible things that involve you being in prison for twenty years or so. So when a student decides it is time for them to part company with you, the best thing you can do is, no matter what the reason is, to give them your blessing and send them on their merry way - its also much less traumatic for all people concerned.

It is really sad, because if you don't do that what usually happens is that the student has outgrown you, essentially, and that doesn't necessarily mean the student now knows more than the teacher. What it means is the student has come to a point where that relationship is no longer of benefit to them, and so they move on to continue their journey. It is a natural part of life and because the student is moving away, they generally get over it a lot quicker, so even when things go bad, they say "ah whatever", and they just sever ties and go on their way, which leaves the teacher being bitter and dwelling on the whole process, which means that the students who remain get a really bad deal. Because instead of being taught, they end up having to listen to the teacher pissing and moaning about the student that left, and it usually spills out into the wider community.

Basically it ends up with a witch war, because when you can't let go of somebody, you tend to attack, because you get so caught up in the emotion of it. You tend to start saying bad things about them in public, and it gets really nasty and it affects the whole local community, and that really is totally unnecessary because all you have to do is say "ok, I'll let you go."

But there are teachers, who are otherwise very good, who just can't seem to do that, which is a real shame The important thing to remember is that even the worst teacher can still do some good, if it is only as a way of acting as a filter - those teachers that don't know anything, but put out a big shiny light and attract lots of students to them, well sooner or later those students are going to come to their senses and move on to a better teacher or they're not, then they are going to stay there following their guru with wide eyes and empty heads, and quite frankly that I see as a service.

Because the students that came to their senses and moved on are wiser, because now they know the sort of teacher to avoid, and so they have developed that discernment, which is very important. The students who choose to stay are obviously not going to do very well on a path that requires discernment, personal responsibility and thinking for yourself, and so by staying with that teacher who has nothing to offer, they aren't bothering the teachers who do have something to offer, leaving those teachers free to teach the students that are willing to put the effort in.

So ultimately it all works out, and hopefully in your path you will notice the pitfalls and avoid them for the most part. Sometimes you're going to step in dog doo, and it just teaches you to learn to see it from further away, so all experiences are learning experiences the bad ones and the good, the trick is to actually learn from them and not to repeat them.

αngels and demons

Episode 72, broadcast on July 19, 2007

Hello and welcome to the Crooked Path, I'm Peter Paddon and while Raven talks about Mistletoe this week I'll be taking a look at Angels and Demons, music is of course by Wendy Rule.

Who are these angels and demons of which I speak, and what's made me want to speak about them? Well this is episode 72 of the crooked path, and 72 of course in Kabbala is the number of Archangels and the number of Names of God, and so - not that I do Kabbala - but it just seemed a feeble excuse really to talk about other entities, mythical creatures, Angels, Demons so on and so forth, other than gods, that we might encounter on the Crooked Path. So basically its a very trite excuse for an attempt at a clever title, which actually covers a multitude of sins, because I'm going to talk about a few different things.

First of all lets take a look at Angels. Now Angels - well we're not talking about your Biblical choirboys here, you know, the dudes in white with the golden wings, all pretty and glowing about the head, announcing the birth of the Messiah, and wielding flaming swords to keep you out of the Garden of Eden, that sort of thing.

Well, the flaming sword thing is a bit more in keeping with the kind of Angels that I have in mind, because Angels weren't like that - the Biblical faiths have kind of sweetened up the Angels to a certain extent, and Christianity has really sapified them to such an extent that any self respecting Angel isn't going to go near a Christian Church, because of the "schmaltzyness" of the nature of Christian Angels.

They were really the hard boys, the enforcers of the esoteric multiverse, if you like, in olden times, and they were known to... you know, they come from Sumerian, Enochian, Egyptian mythology.

The Egyptians knew them as Kerubs, if you follow the taxonomy that the Golden Dawn practiced, and you find them depicted, and described in Sumerian sacred writings quite frequently, and they really really have very little to do with the Christian concept of Angels.

You can't really speak about them without talking about Demons ,or Daemons, as well, Angels are personified forces of nature of the universe. For want of a better description, they are the higher plane equivalents of natures spirits, I guess is one way of looking at it, and it is probably the "poncification" of nature spirits that led to the "poncification" of Angels as well. They have very very clearly defined areas of operation and they cannot do anything outside of those, and their names are actually Hekas, the Names or Words of Power, if you pronounce them correctly, to invoke the energies of the realm or the thing they control.

As I said, you will find them in Sumerian myths, you'll find them in Ancient Egyptian mythology as the servitors of the sons of Horus, so they tend to be very elemental in nature, very two dimensional characters, but very powerful as well. Even in Biblical times - we're talking Old Testament here, rather than New Testament - the angels had some pretty impressive abilities. I mean, the best known one after Gabriel, who really let the side down, would be the Archangel Metatron, who was known as the Voice of God. Anyone whose seen Dogma will remember that whole thing with Alan Rickman being the Voice of God, and doing a pretty darn fine job of it too.

So the thing with Angels is that they are very two dimensional, as I said, very unforgiving... you call on them to do a job that is within their purvey, because outside of that they ain't no good. The classical Archangels of the circle in Kabbalistic, Golden Dawn style workings, and in Gardenarian and Alexandrian Craft as well, are:

Raphael the Archangel of Air
Gabriel the Archangels of Water

Michael the Archangel of Fire
Uriel the Archangel of Earth

Unfortunately there are a lot of typos out there in bookland, and quite often Uriel is written as Auriel, which is actually quite a different Archangel, and calling Auriel in to work the element of Earth ain't gonna do you no good, so it is a good idea to get it right

Other Archangels that are well known... well you have, let me see, well Auriel is the Angel of Death, of course, which puts a whole different slant on your circle if you call him in when you are supposed to be calling Uriel. The really interesting thing about Archangels is that they are... as I said before their names are actually Hekas - their names are Barbarous Words of Power, if you pronounce them right, and especially in Enochian magic this is a very precise science. For example, taking Michael, the Archangel of the South, of fire in the Golden Dawn system, pronounced Michael in Hebrew and when you actually intone it as a word of power Mee-Kai-Ell-Ah, and pronouncing them, intoning them, incanting them that way, makes a profound difference.

If you have a habit of using the Lesser Banishing Ritual as an example - even though it isn't part of the Crooked Path, it isn't part of traditional witchcraft, its a good example of using angelic energies, and so I'm going to be talking about that just for the sake of comparison and practicality when we do the praxis session.

So you would call on Angels for very specific tasks that fall within their remit, so you basically you have to know who it is you are calling and what they are good at, so that you call the right one. Demons are an interesting subset - they are all almost identical to Angelic beings... they are essentially angelic beings themselves . They are often described as demi-gods and great spirits and some traditions even refer to them as the lesser gods, and although the term demon has come to mean a sort of "Spawn of Satan" type

179

thing in modern western society, the actual root was Daemon which has an extra a in there - D A E M O N. This is actually more ambivalent in that "Daemon" can be good or evil, and in fact the old traditional image of the angel on your right shoulder and the demon on your left is they would of both been Daemons in the old days.

Classically Daemons were your inspiration, your mentors, your guides, your guardians if you like there were certain traditions where you had one of each that would promote the good, and one would promote the bad, and thats when that particular image - which has been much used and abused over the centuries - came into being, and the really interesting thing with Daemons is that they do tend to be very personal.

There are some big-arsed Daemons which you can work with, a very good example, one that is actually very important in the world of Traditional Witchcraft, is Azazel also known as Samael the Fallen Angel, and he is something of a poster boy for Traditional Witchcraft. Azazel/Samael is one of the entities that is often referred to as the Witch Father, or the Horned Lord, in certain particular traditions, and once again the name Azazel or even Sammael are Hekas - they are Words of Power that, when you intone them or incant them in the correct way, will summon the energy that they represent, and so this can be a very potent way of working, using Angel and Demon names as incantations.

Other Spirits that you might encounter on your journey along the Crooked Path... well we're always talking about the ancestors so it won't be any surprise to find them here as well. Ancestors are any non-incarnate spirit of your culture and/or family, and because we tend to work in a non-linear sense time-wise when we are in our sacred space, they can be past, present or future. So theres some interesting interactions that can be had there, if you work with Ancestors, and as we've talked about them at length in the past,

I'm not going to sort of spend any more time on them this time round.

There are also guides, spirits that act as mentors for you. They may be your Daemons, they may be your personal inspiration, your muse. They may be guides, guardians that have been sent to you by tutelory deities that you may work with, your Patron and Matron for example, and various other disincarnate spirits that may come along to teach you a specific thing that you may encounter in your journeys exploring realms.

Guardians of realms, Genius Loci, spirits of place, are something that you will encounter if you work outdoors, out in the countryside, you will encounter the spirits of the places that you are working, and they will be more or less hostile, depending upon the nature of humanity's interaction with nature in the area that you are. It doesn't hurt to bring an offering of whisky, or something like that, to share with them, to show them that you mean well, and to gain at least some trust that perhaps they will share with you and help you to enhance your working in the wild as it were.

So theres all sorts of entities out there... mythological beasties I'm going to save for another time. We talked about drakes a bit in the past, but there are a lot of other interesting creatures that may be examined symbolically, metaphorically, or as personifications of certain types of energy and certain types of experience, so we will talk about those on other occasions.

As I was saying in the Lore section Angelic names, Demonic names, Daemonic names if you will, can all be used as Hekas, Words of Power or, as the Golden Dawn initiates used to like calling them, Barbarous Words of Power - you have to say that with a Scottish accent or it just doesn't work... Barbarous! But anyway, thats me being silly, I apologize for that.

So as I said before, the Hebrew angel names Michael, Gabriel, Uriel and Raphael are all pronounced in such a way they become Words of Power, and the same applies to Enochian.

Now, Enochian isn't a system that is frequently used within Traditional Witchcraft, although I know there are some family trads that do use Enochian - technically they wouldn't be called Traditional Witchcraft, because they are a lot more ceremonial in nature, and I think the few family traditions that actually truly deserve the name tend to be a little more ceremonial in nature, and tend to work within a Rosicrucian/Christian mystical sort of framework. So Enochian sometimes comes up amongst them because they tend to take the ceremonial route.

Enochian - the entire language is Words of Power, so its a very interesting thing. So what I'm going to do is go over the Lesser Banishing Ritual of the Pentagram, from the Golden Dawn, in two versions, one using the Hebrew names and one using the Enochian, just to show you the way the words are used, the way that the words are incanted to make them vibratory tones that will work with the energy.

Obviously theres a lot of hand waving, drawing pentagrams and stuff which goes with it, which you can't see because this podcast is an audio only medium, and I may at some point decide to add a video version of this just for the hell of it. But right now I'm not planning to, so if you are familiar with the lesser banishing ritual with a pentagram from the Golden Dawn you can probably supply the imagery for yourself, if not, its not really important for the context in which I am doing this, I just want you to listen to the words and then, you can hopefully get an idea.

It is just basically a use of ritual sonics, and that part at least can be applied, because you can actually find through more intuitive means a way of pronouncing pretty much any entity's name, right up to Deities - and yourself for that matter - to turn them into

Words of Power, and so this is just a little primer if you like.

The Hebrew version of the lesser banishing ritual starts with the Qabalistic Cross, and the words that are said roughly translate as "for you are the kingdom, the power and the glory for ever and ever amen." Those of you that have had any Christian upbringing may recognize that as the end of the Our Father Prayer, the paternoster, and then it goes on to call the four Archangels of the Elements in the four quarters, using Golden Dawn quarters of course and the whole thing sounds something like this...

Ateh, Malkuth, Ve-gevura, Ve-gedula, Le-Olahm, Amen

before me Raphael
behind me Gabriel
on my right hand Michael
on my left hand Uriel

Around me flames the pentagram, and above me shines the six-rayed star

Ateh, Malkuth, Ve-gevura, Ve-gedula, Le-Olahm, Amen

So that's the Hebrew version, and then there is the Enochian version. Now the Enochian version has a slight difference because instead of the Qabalistic Cross, you actually do a pentagram upon your own body that starts with the forehead down to the left breast up to the right shoulder over to the left shoulder down to the right breast and back up to the forehead again, the words mean the same for you are the kingdom the power and the glory for ever and ever amen, but they are in fact Enochian, so you get :

Zoh-Ah Oh-Enn-Doh, Mee-Hey, Boo-Zoh-Day, Pah-Ee-Day

And then the four angels of the four quarters are called:

> Before me Iczhikal (Ee-Keh-Zod-Hee-Kal)
> Behind me Edlprnaa (eh-Del-Par-Nah-Ah)
> On my right Raagiosl (Rah-Ah-Gee-Oh-Sel)
> On my left Bataivah (Bah-Tah-Ee-Vah-Heh)

> Behold the four flaming pentagrams, and I alone in the center.

So that is intoning angelic names as Words of Power, as Hekas and if you do it in full ritual, it actually raises quite a lot of oomph in a rather nice way. There is a definite difference in feel to the energy of doing it Hebrew or Enochian, The Enochian one is very cold and clinical, in fact the whole Enochian magical system is very cold and clinical but quite efficient and hopefully that has given you a few ideas on ways to play with sound.

I know that we... my own group has taken the techniques that are involved in that little ritual, and have extrapolated, modified and worked with it, and used our intuition and tapping the bone to find ways of using it in different forms, within our own traditional crafting, and its been a very interesting journey. So I thought I'd give you the seeds, as it were, so that you can go and play with it and perhaps start a journey of your own, looking at sounds and entities in your crafting.

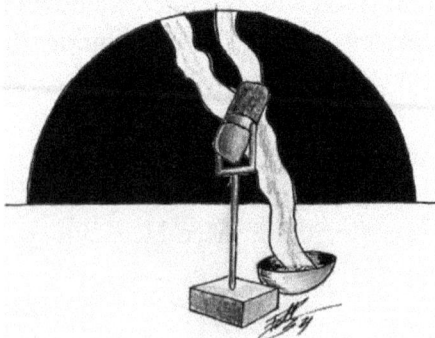

I'm Just Saɟin'
Episode 93, broadcast on March 7, 2008

Hello and welcome to the Crooked Path. My name is Peter Paddon and this week I will be interviewing Ann Finnin, author of the new book The Forge of Tubal Cain. But first, I'm going to look inward for a bit and share some of the whys and wherefores of this podcast ,and what other people have been saying about us.

I guess calling this section lore is a little bit of a stretch this time, but we're going to be looking inwards quite a lot this time around. We're going to be looking at why it is exactly I do this show, what I'm hoping to get out of it, and what some of the reactions have been, what sort of impact it's having on the big wide world out there.

I was actually quite surprised to find that it is apparently having an impact; sometimes positive, sometimes negative, but certainly I seem to have got people talking a little bit which is probably a good thing. For example, there's a traditional witchcraft forum, I'm not going to name any names in any of this because people are pissed at me enough already I guess, but there's a traditional witchcraft forum in the UK that has been talking about me. I came up in a discussion, a thread, about the black spirits and white, red spirits and gray stuff, and got interestingly lumped in with Robin Artisson.

Both of us got described as providing Traditional Witchcraft "for the masses", a sort witchcraft-lite if you like, based on the fact that we mostly talk about four directions whereas everybody who is involved in Traditional Witchcraft knows there are generally more directions than that, and they're not the classical elements, and so on and so forth.

Somebody latched onto the show where I talked about the black spirits and white, red spirits and gray stuff and, first of all decided that, well they did have the grace to say they hoped that our private practice involved more than that - which it does - but that we were being very Wiccan in talking about four directions.

Well, I don't know about you, but I follow an initiatory tradition and the stuff that we learn and teach and share is layered, and you don't give everybody all the layers at once. You start with a simple basic outline, if you like, and then you fill it in. When you get to a certain point you get to say "oh, there's this overlay over it" and you start to fill that in and that keeps on going on forever basically.

So, I just wanted to say that I'm not trying to portray "trad-lite" in any sense of the word with this podcast, it's just that you've got to start somewhere, and it seems simplest to start with a circle cross as my "diagram of the day", if you like, and start off by talking about a sort of nominally quarter-based system and then layer stuff on as it becomes apparent that it's time to move a little deeper and start bring the other layers - and the other directions - and all the other stuff in as well. If I jumped in at the deep end and started talking about everything all at once it would just be the gobbledygook podcast and nobody would enjoy that. So, I just wanted to make that clear. The little poem itself:

Black spirits and white,
Red spirits and gray,
Come ye, come ye, come ye what may.
Thout a tout tout,
Around and about,
The good stay in and the ill stay out.

And so on and so forth; yes it is from Shakespeare and what's the problem with that? Shakespeare was a good researcher. He used a lot of stuff that he found that he found that was in folklore of the time, in the Elizabethan age, and some of the stuff he picked up has been identified as stuff that is genuinely of interesting esoteric focus at the time.

He was a man of his season, a man of his time, and a lot of the stuff that he pulled in were what was going on around him. So just because Shakespeare put it in a play doesn't mean it can't possibly have been used by Traditional Witches or any other sort of magical person at the time. In fact I'm inclined to believe that there's quite a lot of good lore in Shakespeare and if you just discount it as "oh, it's a playwright, it's a play, it's fiction" then you're kind of missing the point in my opinion.

I found it very interesting; there were some interesting comments along the side in that conversation, lumping the podcast and Pendraig Publishing in together. One dear lady decided to lay into Pendraig Publishing with "nobody's ever heard of any of their authors" and it's a nasty, "naff" website, and two of their supposed authors do this podcast - referring to this one (The Crooked Path) of course, and referring to Raven and myself - and how awful we are. She cited in particular, at one point in a recent podcast I asked Raven what her number one tip for making incense was and she basically said something along the lines of don't burn stuff that's bad for you, and apparently this person who is commenting has no sense of humor and doesn't realize when people are joking. And even in the joke is actually a good point; don't burn stuff that's bad for you boys and girls. It was just absolutely hilarious.

There's another person on another UK forum who decided that this podcast sounds way too much like bad late night local radio chat shows to be worth listening to. So, for that person, although they won't be listening, "the time now is quarter past the hour, and..." yeah, I won't go there, except I already have, so sorry folks.

Then I came across an interesting discussion on a Hindu website actually, not Indian Hindu, but I guess North American Hindu, western folk doing eastern stuff type website, where there was a discussion about reincarnation. Somebody had brought up my podcast on Cosmic Soup and the Mighty Dead, and the idea of people being recycled into the mix, and it's only the Mighty Dead that get to reincarnate as discreet individuals. I found this particularly interesting because they were basically pulling apart my Celtic perspective from a standpoint of their New Age Hindu perspective, along with comments like "I'm not even sure that Celts believed in reincarnation".

Well, it doesn't take a lot of research to find that they do, or did rather, and that the whole Cauldron-born, Mighty Dead thing is classic Celt, especially Welsh Celt, reincarnation theory. It kind of bothered me, not that they were picking me apart cause I'm kind of used to that at this point, but that they seemed to have a profound lack of understanding of their own system because they couldn't see any correlation at all and they seem to have totally dismissed one of the prime tenets of the more prevalent form of Hindu belief in reincarnation, that the average person does not reincarnate as a discreet individual. The soul is multi-faceted and each facet reincarnates as part of a different being.

So it's kind of like the cosmic soup except they see them all as coming back together in between lives to amalgamate the experiences. It's a case of doing multiple reincarnations at the same time to increase the speed of your learning, if you like, and they seem to have totally dismissed that, and not be able to get their heads around that concept at all. So they're working with a very simplified, westernized version of reincarnation. Well, ok, a westernized version of an eastern belief in reincarnation; and then managing to totally miss the ball when comparing it to an actual western form of reincarnation. I just found the whole thing very entertaining.

I have to admit, some of the comments on some of the sites have been a little... they got to me a little. I'm a very thin-skinned individual, so I found some of the nastier jibes to be a little painful, but the Hindu one, it just amused me because it was just so really fun.

So, that brings us really to the point of why exactly do I do this? I had originally started out this podcast, two years ago, basically to promote my DVDs. I saw it as a way of putting out very little money and getting some publicity for them. That was the original intent, and it hasn't worked out that way, in case you hadn't guessed. In the early podcasts I used to put in ads for my DVD's, I've pretty much stopped doing that now because it seemed to make absolutely no difference. The reason I've continued to do the podcasts, and the reason that I'm now paying in excess of $100 a month for a dedicated server to make sure that the podcast stays up, even when everybody decides to download an episode at once, is that basically I love doing it.

I have a very strong need to provide service, it's part of the path I walk. I used to do that by teaching classes at Raven's Flight, in Raven's store in North Hollywood before she went totally online, and when her store closed I never really found anywhere that I felt right continuing that. The other stores were... pretty much all of them are too far away to be practical to get to on a weekday evening anyway, and I just never felt at home teaching at any of them. I guess after seven years of teaching at Raven's Flight, I was rather used to the place.

So, this podcast and to a lesser extent my DVDs, have replaced that face-to-face classroom opportunity for me. This is now my place where I provide service to the community. This is where I fulfill that need, that obligation within myself, and everything you hear from me is basically coming from where I am. I'm not a person who believes in or enjoys playing politics, or trying to mask things, or being a trickster, or anything like that. Despite there being some people in the world that seem to think that I am evil incarnate, the Pagan equivalent of the anti-Christ if you will, I actually like to think I'm a pretty sincere person.

When I say this is why I'm doing this podcast, generally speaking I'm being totally up front with you, I don't tend to hide my motivations at all really. I do try to avoid hurting people's feelings, I try to be polite, and I will attempt to be diplomatic upon occasion, but aside from that pretty much everything you get from me is shooting straight from the hip and can be taken at face value.

It really tends to amaze me, and it's a very painful experience, when people don't accept that, and they think that I'm trying to be deceitful or trying to manipulate, and stuff like that, because really I'm just trying to share - I think is the best way to describe it. I'm trying to share things that have become very important to me in my life, and I'm going to continue doing that. I'm not going to let anything anybody says change the way I feel, or change the way that I follow through on my need to do this. So this podcast isn't going anywhere and neither am I basically[1].

So that is the whole raison d'être of why I'm doing this, and some of the feedback that hasn't been officially given to us. The comments I get on Podcast Alley and various other places are absolutely wonderful, and they really boost my spirit and make me feel that this is something that is important in people's lives and so I want to continue doing it for that as well. But some of these unsolicited comments that I come across, while some of them are hurtful and distress me a little, there's nothing that tells me I don't want to do it. In fact in some cases, some of the comments that I come across that are negative actually spur me on to do it more, because I'm obviously having an impact if I can make curmudgeonly old women in the UK feel the need to lay into me verbally on a forum that I don't attend. I'm having an impact; let's hope overall the impact is positive.

---

1 Of course, the time did come, in June of 2009, when I felt I had no choice to discontinue the Crooked Path website. But I still do podcasts on the Pendraig website.

190

Interview with Ann Finnin

Peter: Here I am with Ann Finnin, who is the author of the brand spanking new book *The Forge of Tubal Cain²*, everything that you ever wanted to know about the Clan of Tubal Cain, 1734, and the Roebuck Tradition, but were afraid to ask. Hi Ann, how you doing?

Ann Finnin: Hello Peter.

Peter: So, let's start off by learning a little bit about your new book.

Ann: Well, it was a chronicle of the journey that we took from first getting into the Craft, and the people that we knew, and the experiences we had through trying to discover our own tradition, and how we could make it work in the modern world, and some of the experiences we had trying to make it work, and some of the pitfalls and some of the people that helped us make it work over the years. So it's a story, not just of a tradition, but of a group and of a mystery school that we hoped would take the teachings and expand on them and hopefully carry them on to a new generation.

Peter: What made you decide to start writing the book?

Ann: Well we had been asked some years back by various students about the history of the group, who we studied with, who influenced us, where we got some of the things that we used in our circles, and I got the idea of writing it down as a sort of chronicle, as more of a memoir than a serious history to give students an idea of where we came from and who we studied with. So much of the early Craft scene that we discovered was shrouded in mystery, and they learned it from their grandmother or they had some secret writing

2   *The Forge of Tubal Cain*, published by Pendraig.

from somewhere. We thought that our students deserved to know who taught us and where we got our information so that they could take that and add to it and pass it along.

Peter: That's really cool. So despite your youthful looks, you've been around in the Pagan scene for a while now. What would you say has surprised you the most about the way the Craft has changed in the last god knows how many years?

Ann: Well, now it seems to be a lot less centralized. Back in the day, if you wanted to learn anything about the craft there were very few books. The ones that were available were older and harder to read. The only way of learning how to do magic, and learning Craft, was by joining a coven, usually taught by a teacher that had some kind of mandate from some authority to pass on a tradition. So that was how you learned. Now you've got the internet, you've got tons of books, and a variety of teachers and gurus and High Priestesses and Witch Queens and everybody, that there's no reason to join an established authority, you can kind of learn it on your own. So you have a lot of people who are practicing Craft without being part of a coven or part of a tradition.

Peter: What would you say was the hardest thing about writing this book?

Ann: Well, so much of our early history involved being, not, well lied to is a little strong, but trying to have the wool pulled over our eyes. People spouting spurious authorities and "oh we got it from our grandmother" or "oh this tradition is unchanged since the middle ages" and "oh its ancient writing, that you're not supposed to change one word of" and all this. When we found out that it was not true and that these myths and these stories were being perpetrated

192

by people who basically didn't know any more than we did, but wanted to establish their own egos and power trips, there was some disillusionment and a big temptation to say that the emperor has no clothes and be rather more ruthless about it than perhaps was charitable. I had to tone down an awful lot of the accusations and the revelations and the fact that so and so really wasn't who they said they were, and present the information in such a way that it revealed the truth without being snarky.

Peter: So there is room for a limited edition unrated version.

Ann: Well there has been. There has been over the years privately printed comments and commentaries and memoirs and things that tell more than the book does, but I try to preserve the spirit of the thing and leave out a lot of the names of people because the names of people I discovered weren't all that important. What was important was all of the pitfalls that the student, the seeker, the searcher, can run into. There were a lot of people that did the same thing, so if you can uncover the patterns without sticking names on them then you don't pillory people who perhaps shouldn't be pilloried at this point.

Peter: That's a very good viewpoint to take. So, have you saved some juicy details for a sequel?

Ann: Oh yes. The story is just beginning in many ways. We've told the story of The Roebuck and our journey in establishing the tradition, but there is more. When we explored the history behind The Clan of Tubal Cain and some of the adventures we had with uncovering that tradition and some of the people that we met over the course of the years and the people that helped us and the people that hindered us, so there's more.

193

Peter: Very cool. Now the book includes material about Roebuck practice, would you say it's a fairly comprehensive introduction to the work of your coven?

Ann: It's a good theoretical introduction. Most of the work that we do is very visionary, very shamanic, and very individual. A lot of it depends on who's in the circle, who's doing the work, so the techniques are going to vary depending on who's doing it. We learn by doing rather than by having a cookbook of instructions. I tended to want to concentrate on the theory of why we do what we do rather than what actually we do, because it's going to be different for everybody, and you can't really use it as an instruction manual but it does give the philosophy behind it, and the reasons why we've instituted some of the techniques that we use.

Peter: Aside from the juicy sequel, do you have any plans for any other books?

Ann: Well, I've been trying to get some fiction published over the last several years and I've been heartened that over the last 5-6 years the publishing world in general has discovered Paganism and the Craft and Goddess religion, and you see on the shelves not just fantasy and science fiction, but romance and mysteries that all deal with Pagan type themes.

It seems like the mainstream publishers are starting to discover us, so maybe there will a market for pagan themed fiction. That would be something that I'd like to get into. I'm not very sure if the sorts of things that I've written in The Forge of Tubal Cain or any of those other books to follow is mainstream enough, but maybe the market will change and maybe there will be more of a niche for how magic and the occult is done on a day to day basis rather than on a fantasy basis.

Peter: Very cool. Well thank you very much Ann. It might be biased of me to say this because I am, in fact, your publisher, but I'm going to say it anyway because it's true - thoroughly enjoyed the book, thoroughly enjoyed putting it together for you and I think it's going to be around for a while.

Ann: It was a labor of love and I tried very hard to make it a good read...

Peter: You've certainly succeeded.

Ann: ...and an exciting story, and hope everyone who reads it will enjoy the story all the more for it being a true one.

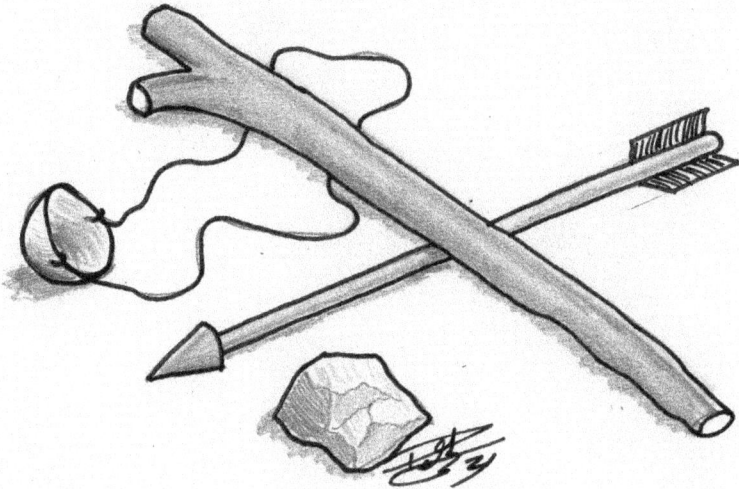

Index